D1232171

DETROIT PUBLIC LIBRARY

CHANEY BRANCH LIBRARY
16101 GRAND RIVER
DETROIT, MI 48227

DATE DUE

BC-3

JAN - - 2003

# A GOOD SOUP ATTRACTS CHAIRS

## A First African Cookbook for American Kids

## FRAN OSSEO-ASARE

### With help from
### Abena, Masi, and D.K.

PELICAN PUBLISHING COMPANY
Gretna 2001

Copyright © 1993
By Fran Osseo-Asare
All rights reserved

*The word "Pelican" and the depiction of a pelican are trademarks of Pelican Publishing Company, Inc., and are registered in the U.S. Patent and Trademark Office.*

All photos courtesy of Fran Osseo-Asare.

**Library of Congress Cataloging-in-Publication Data**

Osseo-Asare, Fran.
    A good soup attracts chairs : a first African cookbook for American kids / Fran Osseo-Asare with help from Abena, Masi, and D.K.
        p.    cm.
    Summary: Presents over thirty-five easy-to-follow recipes from the kitchens of West Africa and Ghana and instructions on how to throw an African party.

    1. Cookery, West African—Juvenile literature. 2. Cookery—Ghana—Juvenile literature. 3. Entertaining—Juvenile literature. [1. Cookery, African.]    I. Title.
TX725.W47084 1993
641.5966—dc20                                                    92-42982
                                                                      CIP
                                                                       AC

Manufactured in the United States of America
Published by Pelican Publishing Company, Inc.
1000 Burmaster Street, Gretna, Louisiana 70053

*This book is dedicated to the memory of the two African women who have influenced my life the most profoundly:*

*Janet Akosua Agyepoma Osseo-Asare*
*1922-1959*

*and her daughter*
*Eunice Afua Ahyi Osseo-Asare*
*1954-1992*

# Contents

# Acknowledgments

To name all of the people who have contributed substantively to this book would double its length. The testers know who they are: Abena, Masi, and DK's elementary, junior high, and high school friends; Kim Mitchell's third-grade class; the local Girl Scouts; the Cooperative Playschool's staff and alumni; patrons at Schlow Memorial Library; my Sunday school class; and friends and relatives scattered across the country. I am grateful to you all.

Some of my many mentors and teachers know who they are as well: Joseph Kwamena Okyere (my first Twi and cooking instructor in Berkeley), Beatrice Larbi, Theodora Osseo-Asare, Naana Nti, Abenaa Owusu, Alice Opare, Dora Barnafo, and Beryl Adu. Others, such as cooks and roadside vendors, remain anonymous; but my debt and gratitude to them is not lessened. Thank you to each of you—named and unnamed.

The technical and emotional support provided by my community at University Mennonite Church was instrumental in seeing this project through. Special thanks go to Joel and Krista Weidner, Becky Nordvall, Vicki Markley-Sairs, and Susie Wenger.

I benefited greatly from Marc Levey's instruction—as well as my classmates' helpful comments—on both the creative and technical aspects of food photography.

My warmest acknowledgment is reserved for my favorite critic, my exacting but enthusiastic teacher, my generous funding source, and the original inspiration for the learning behind this book—Kwadwo. Finally, I thank my coworkers and long-suffering offspring, Abena, Masi, and D.K. Lee, for their endless help and encouragement. Remember, "Little by little, the chicken drinks water."

Pelican Publishing Company and editor Nina Kooij endured the disruptions of my several trips abroad and the writing of my doctoral dissertation, which delayed the completion of this manuscript. I acknowledge with gratitude their patience and flexibility.

This book was born seven years ago, during the prayer of my four-year-old son. In 1985, after watching a television news story about the suffering of children in Ethiopia, he prayed that God would help hurting children in Africa. After he prayed, I told him that God asks us to bring our few fish to Him, and He blesses them and multiplies them to feed others. I then promised to write this book. We agreed as a family that any profits coming from it would be used to help hungry children in Africa. I acknowledge my son's childlike faith and God's faithfulness in seeing me through the completion of the task. We will keep our promise.

# Our Family and Africa

People call the United States a "melting pot" of heritages and cultures; but they don't mean it in the sense that you throw ten kinds of wax into a kettle and melt them down into one big blob. It is more like the "stone soup" legend, in which everybody brings what they have and adds it to the pot, and the resulting soup is a wonderful blend of tastes and textures and seasonings.

My own family is an example of such a "stone soup" of traditions. For example, my grandfather—my father's father— was from Norway. He told me nursery rhymes in Norwegian and taught me to jump over a broomstick. He also ate flatbread and sardines, and poured his coffee into the saucer to cool it. Dad was born in Montana, then his family moved to a farm in Oregon. My mother's side of the family was Scotch-Irish. Mom was born in Tennessee and grew up in Appalachia. I never met her father, who was a logger and had a special way with wild animals. Her mother was a wonderful seamstress and herbalist. I was born in the Pacific Northwest and grew up in the San Francisco Bay Area during the 1950s and 1960s. There I learned something about the Mexican, Chinese, Italian, and Japanese contributions to America. To me, that first meant foods—from tacos and enchiladas to pasta, eggrolls, and sukiyaki. Later, in college, I learned about Indian curries and Middle Eastern pitas and kebabs. When my mother married my stepfather, I gained a French connection; but that is another story.

This melting pot cooking tale begins later. It is the story of an adventure that began over twenty years ago in California, then moved to Africa and continues today in central Pennsylvania and beyond.

It was in 1968, at the University of California in Berkeley, that I became friends with a student from Ghana. I had never heard of Ghana before then. It is one of the countries along the western coast of sub-Saharan Africa. Before it became independent from the British in 1957, it had been known as the Gold Coast due to the large amount of gold there. It was also famous for its "black gold"—the cocoa that it produced and

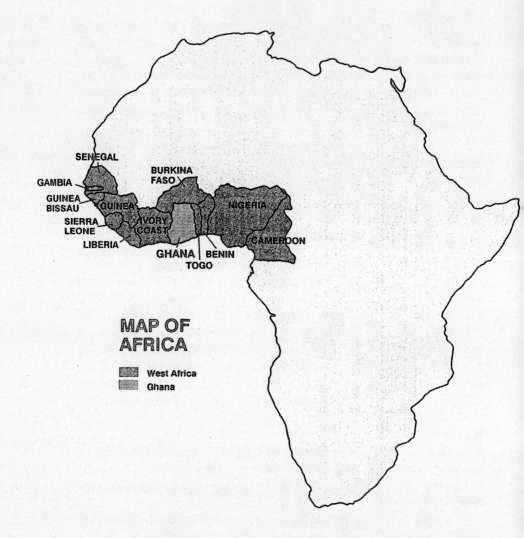

SENEGAL

GAMBIA

GUINEA
BISSAU

GUINEA

SIERRA
LEONE

LIBERIA

BURKINA
FASO

IVORY
COAST

GHANA

TOGO

BENIN

NIGERIA

CAMEROON

## MAP OF AFRICA

West Africa
Ghana

sent to places like Hershey, Pennsylvania. Additionally, it was one of the main points through which slaves passed from Africa to the New World.

Well, the friendship between me and the young man from Ghana grew over several years into love. We decided to marry, but first I wanted to spend a year in Ghana to get to know his people, his country, and especially the food that he was raised on. In 1971, I went alone to Ghana. I lived and taught school in a small fishing village on the coast. That experience was many things, but mostly it was the discovery of a hospitable people and their very good food.

I learned that the food was not as strange as I had imagined it would be. There is an important link between West African cooking and our own Southern cooking—a link forged largely by the slave trade. *Gumbo* is a Bantu word for okra, and *yam* is a West African word. Okra, peanuts, sesame, and black-eyed peas were all introduced into the American diet by African slaves—most of whom came from West Africa. Watermelon is also originally from Africa. Gumbos, "greens," and one-pot rice meals like jambalaya strikingly resemble West African soups and stews. The use of deep frying and spicy seasonings are both important in West African cuisine.

At the end of my year in Ghana, my boyfriend met me there and we were married in 1972 before returning to the United States for more schooling. It was in the U.S. that our three children—Abena, Masi, and D.K.—were born. Abena spent her first six months in Colorado; and Masi and D.K. were born and are growing up in central Pennsylvania. In 1984, they had their first real taste of life in Africa when our family spent four months in a small town in Ghana. There the children learned to appreciate many new foods. One day we were in a land of hamburgers and pizza and apples; and two days later, we were eating soup and *fufu*, jollof rice, and papaya.

By the time we returned to the United States, African (Ghanaian) foods were very much a part of our lives—we even began to notice a ripple effect spreading out to our extended family and friends. People were interested and curious about African cooking—from local nursery and elementary schools,

Girl Scout troops, and church members to as far away as cousins André and Jacques in Oregon. Kids we knew were cracking coconuts and frying twisted cakes and sampling peanut butter stew and *kelewele*. It was and still is exciting.

This brings us to this latest part of the story. When I first wanted to teach our children what I had learned about Ghanaian cooking in the courtyards of African family and friends, I had little help that was written down. That is probably because cooking is still an oral tradition in Africa in which children learn how to cook from their mothers or aunts, and recipes are usually not written down especially for children. After we came back to Pennsylvania, we realized that little material on African cooking was available for American children. Some of what existed in international cookbooks was amusing, such as substituting American sweet potatoes for West African yams to make fufu. (To understand why this was amusing, see the entry for yams in the glossary of ingredients.) The lack of American material might be partially due to the fact that historically few Americans have traveled to sub-Saharan Africa and learned to enjoy and appreciate African foods.

At any rate, the children were enthusiastic and Mother was willing, so we decided to put together this cookbook. The recipes included are Ghanaian, which represents only a glimpse into one of the infinite varieties of cooking—even within West Africa. There are differences, for instance, between Anglophone (English-speaking) and Francophone (French-speaking) West Africa, depending on whether the countries were English or French colonies. However, although some of the recipes are specific to Ghana, many of those we chose are found with variations throughout sub-Saharan Africa. It was important to me to stick with recipes that I know are authentic—foods I learned to eat and prepare in Ghana or from Ghanaians or other West Africans.

All friendships begin with an introduction, and this book is aimed at introducing American kids to African cooking and life in part of Africa. The special links between the West African coast and the American South make cooking an excellent starting point.

# Cooking African

The courtyard is often the kitchen in Ghana, and it plays a similar role to that of the American hearth during our own pioneer days. The courtyard is a collage of sounds, smells, and routines—chickens scratching, a young child fanning charcoal in a brazier, a mother calmly breast-feeding her baby as she stirs bubbling soup, men sitting nearby on stools and joking, children laughing, and smoked fish drying. Earlier in the morning, the mother in charge might have been seen in the outdoor marketplace, skillfully bartering in her stall, her head shaking over neat piles of tomatoes and garden eggs (a relative of the eggplant) or smoked shrimp and rice. Maybe she walked through the market gracefully balancing a huge basket on her brightly kerchiefed head, wearing a long dress made of one of the boldly designed local cloths. Perhaps she was away at work and sent her "house girl" to do the shopping. Regardless, as she sits stirring the soup, there is anticipation on everyone's faces. The delicious aroma of meat, seafood, and vegetables fills the courtyard. In another pot, yams and plantains are boiling.

Although our kitchens are quite different from many of those in Africa, there is no reason why we cannot cook some of the same tasty meals and snacks. Enjoying good food is something everyone likes to do. As the Akan people in Africa say, "A good soup attracts chairs." Actually, the proverb literally translates to "seats," which would probably be the low stools that people sit on rather than chairs, but the idea is the same.

Before you start to cook, some special things need to be said about cooking and eating the African way. This is because the kinds of foods we will cook and the way we will cook them are sometimes different from American foods.

Many African foods are made with onions and hot peppers, both of which need to be handled very carefully. Also, some of the recipes call for ingredients that may be new to you. Finally, many of the recipes are fried or boiled, and it is extra important to be careful around hot oil and steam.

To help you decide which recipe to try, look at the photographs, then look at the recipes. The recipes are divided into three groups:

 easy to prepare—good for beginners

 a little harder—may need an adult helper

 more difficult—for older cooks or with an adult helper

Before you cook:

1. Wash your hands (and maybe put on an apron).
2. Read the whole recipe.
3. Get out all the ingredients and tools that you will need.
4. Make sure that there is an adult around to help.

Always remember:

1. Be very, very careful with sharp knives. Hold a knife by the handle and away from you. Also, curl your fingers in when chopping fruits or vegetables.
2. Have potholders or oven mitts handy and use them.
3. Turn pot handles away from you on the stove, so they don't get knocked over accidentally.
4. Use a timer if you have one.
5. When lifting the lid on a covered pot, tip the lid so the steam will not go into your face or hands.
6. Use long-handled wooden spoons or spatulas whenever possible—the long handles will help protect you from being splattered, and wooden spoons don't get hot when left in a pot or pan.
7. Have dry hands when you plug or unplug electric appliances like fryers or blenders.

# Kitchen Equipment

The following list includes all of the different tools and equipment that we use in our home to prepare the recipes in this book. You may not have all of these, but don't worry. You can often substitute something you do have—like a cake pan for a broiling pan, or a metal colander inside a soup pot to make a steamer insert. Other things, like an ice cream scoop or a vegetable masher, are nice to have, but are not absolutely necessary. Before you begin to cook any of the recipes, ask an adult to help you figure out how to substitute if you don't have some of the equipment.

**Bowls:** It is good to have a variety of different sizes of bowls for mixing ingredients or serving foods. We have mostly stainless steel mixing bowls and ovenproof bowls and casserole dishes.

**Broiling/baking pans:** A broiling pan is a flat pan that is a few inches deep that you can put in the oven right under the broiler to cook meat or vegetables, like *Chichinga*. Sometimes, like when roasting plantain or baking turnovers, a cookie sheet will work even better because of its lower edges.

**Can opener:** Every kitchen needs a good, sturdy, easy-to-use can opener.

**Cheesecloth:** This is a fine cotton material that looks like gauze. It is used to strain solids from liquids. We use it when we make *Ginger Beer.*

**Colander:** A colander is usually used to drain spaghetti, noodles, or washed lettuce or fruits. It comes in handy for several of the African recipes, like *Ginger Beer,* or as a homemade steamer insert for cooking *Kenkey.* We often drain fried foods in ours as well.

**Cutting board:** It is always important to have something to put on your counter to protect it from sharp knives—whether you are chopping onions or slicing oranges.

**Electric blender:** We use an electric blender in many of the recipes to grind up things like tomatoes, onions, beans, or eggplant. If you do not have an electric blender, you may use a food processor. If you don't have either, you can usually just cut the vegetables into small pieces and add them to the recipe without grinding them.

**Electric deep fryer:** We always use a small electric deep fryer when frying *Plantain Chips, African Doughnuts, Kelewele, Akla,* or *Twisted Cakes.* Our testers who did not have deep fryers used electric skillets or even frying pans. If you are going to deep fry anything—especially if you are not using an electric deep fryer—work side-by-side with an adult, or let the adult do the frying for you. BE CAREFUL. Watch the oil and make sure it does not get too hot and start to smoke. Don't put so much oil or shortening into the fryer or pan that it bubbles up and overflows when you add the food. Don't get splattered in the face when you add the food to the oil, and don't burn your fingers by touching the hot oil.

**Grater:** There are many different kinds of graters, and we use two. Both are hand-held. One is a box with a handle on the top and an open bottom that you can set right on a plate while you grate something. Usually each side grates one or two different sizes—from very fine to very coarse—and one part of the grater will slice vegetables. Another kind of hand-held grater is just a flat piece of metal with a handle at each end. Different parts of the grater will grate finely or coarsely, and the slicer blade is in the middle of the grater. This kind of grater is good for making *Plantain Chips,* but you have to find a way to hold the grater over a plate or bowl with only one hand while holding the plantain with the other hand. I usually push one end of the grater against my body to keep it steady while I grate.

**Hammer:** I have heard of people using an axe to chop open coconuts, but that sounds scary to me. We have always used a hammer.

**Ice cream scoop:** An ice cream scoop is handy for making *Rice Balls.*

**Juicer:** There are many different kinds of juicers for squeezing juice from oranges, limes, and lemons. The simplest type has a plastic or glass part to push the cut half of the fruit against while you turn the fruit, and the juice collects in the bottom. Each time you squeeze half a citrus fruit, you pour the juice out into another container. Others have a larger glass container attached that keeps straining and collecting the juice until you have a cup or two. Even without a juicer, you can squeeze juice from fruit; but it is a lot more work if you want more than a few tablespoons of juice.

**Knives:** We sometimes use table knives, sometimes sharper paring knives, and sometimes large butcher or cutting knives depending on whether we want to cut vegetables, fruits, meat, or fish.

**Measuring cups:** We have glass, plastic, and stainless steel measuring cups in all sizes. Glass measuring cups with spouts are good for liquids, when you need a little extra room to keep the liquid from spilling. The metal or plastic cups are better for dry or chopped ingredients.

**Mixer (electric or hand):** The only recipe in this book that is really easier with a mixer is the *Akla*, and even then you can substitute a wire whisk.

**Pastry brush:** A pastry brush is useful whenever you need to brush something onto something else without making a mess— like brushing oil on pieces of meat when making *Chichinga.*

**Pitchers and jars:** It is good to have pitchers or jars for storing and serving beverages. We recycle old peanut butter and spaghetti jars with screw-on lids for storing the squashes and *Ginger Beer*.

**Potholders:** We have quite a collection of potholders, but we very often end up using folded dishtowels instead.

**Pots and Pans:** It seems to me that every kitchen needs the following: one- and two-quart saucepans, a big soup kettle (at least five quarts), a large pot with a steamer insert, and a ten-inch frying pan—all with lids.

**Rolling pin:** We have a nice wooden rolling pin that we use all the time—whether we are rolling out dough or breaking peanuts into pieces.

**Rubber spatula or scraper:** This is another utensil that is always nice to have for cleaning out bowls and spreading things.

**Sieve or sifter:** When I was growing up, our family always sifted flour with a metal sifter with a handle that you turned to sift the ingredients. In Ghana, I learned to simply shake flour through a fine mesh sieve or strainer to sift it. We have a large sieve that we put over a bowl when making *Ginger Beer* or use to sift flour for *African Doughnuts*, *Twisted Cakes*, or *Fish Turnovers*.

**Strainers:** The metal sieve that I described above is also known as a strainer because the fine wire mesh strains out things. Besides large strainers, this book suggests using smaller strainers. They are helpful, for example, in keeping tea leaves out of tea cups or orange seeds and pulp out of glasses.

**Spoons and paddles:** We use measuring spoons a lot, and sturdy long-handled wooden spoons or flat wooden paddles for stirring soup or stews, *Banku* or *Fufu*. We often use a long-handled slotted spoon for lifting fried foods out of hot oil.

**Timer:** We have an electric timer on our microwave that we use to keep track of how long we have been cooking food. Before we had the microwave, we used a little bell timer.

**Turner:** This is one of the most-used tools in our kitchen. We don't just turn pancakes with our turner. We use it to fry onions and tomatoes and fish and to stir up many different kinds of stews and sauces.

**Vegetable peeler:** This utensil is helpful for peeling potatoes and other vegetables.

**Vegetable masher:** I mashed rice for *Rice Balls* with the side of a wooden spoon until the day I discovered how easy it is to do it with a vegetable masher (also called a potato ricer).

**Wire rack:** This is handy for cooling turnovers.

# Glossary of West African Ingredients

The following ingredients, which are called for in the recipes in this book, might be unfamiliar to you, but most of them can be found in supermarkets if you hunt. A few exceptions are dried lemongrass, agushi, cassava (the only version of cassava used in this book has been processed into gari), gari, palm oil, canned cream of palmnuts, white stone-ground cornmeal, and plantains. Dried lemongrass is an herb that is usually available in health food stores. The agushi, gari, palm oil, canned cream of palm fruits, and cornmeal are often carried by ethnic stores that sell Latin American, West Indian, or African foods. It is easiest to find them in large cities and university towns. We have been able to regularly find plantains in grocery stores in California, Colorado, and Pennsylvania. If you cannot find them, talk to the produce buyers at your local supermarkets. They might be willing to order some for you.

**Agushi:** The Latin name for the seeds of this African watermelon (and the melon itself) is *citrullus colocynthis*, but I first learned to call them *agushi* in Ghana. The more common name in African cookbooks is the Yoruba *egusi* or the Hausa *agusi*. These seeds look a lot like pumpkin seeds, and in Ghana the outer shell of the seed is removed and the whitish seed inside is ground up or roasted. The roasted seeds can be eaten as a snack. The ground seeds are used as thickeners for soups or stews (see the recipe for palaver sauce). If it is hard to find imported agushi, substitutions for thickening soups and stews include (for 1/2 cup agushi): a well-beaten raw egg, two chopped hard-boiled eggs, one cup mashed canned beans, 1/4 cup tapioca flour or instant tapioca, or a cup of peeled and diced eggplant. These substitutions will thicken the sauce, but without the special nutty flavor of agushi. Toasted pumpkin seeds make a substitute snack for roasted agushi seeds.

**Avocado:** The avocado is a fruit that is shaped like a pear, and in Ghana "pear" is its local name in English. Inside a ripe avocado is a yellow, rich buttery fruit. I grew up eating fresh avocados in California; and the Haas variety from California, which is sold throughout the United States in the summertime, is my favorite. Its skin is black and bumpy. Larger avocados with smooth green skins are grown in Florida. Avocados are almost always unripe in the grocery stores, so they must be bought a few days early to allow them to ripen until they are soft, but not mushy. To speed up the ripening process, put one in a bag with a ripe banana or tomato. If the avocado is ripe before you need it, it can be stored in the refrigerator for a couple of days.

**Black-eyed peas:** These light tan beans with a black "eye" on their inner curve are actually dried peas. They originally come from Africa, where they are known as "cowpeas." There are many different kinds and colors of cowpeas, and they are an important source of protein in Africa. They are often cooked in a stew with a little smoked fish, or with rice, or ground and either fried or steamed (see the recipes for Bean Stew, Akla, and Rice and Beans). The tender leaves of the cowpea are also used as a cooked green vegetable.

**Cassava (also called manioc):** A very important food in Africa, cassava is originally from South America and was introduced into Africa by the Portuguese in the seventeenth century. This starchy root's tubers can be peeled and boiled like potatoes, or dried and grated to make a flour (*see* gari). Tapioca is a processed form of cassava that is a good thickener that is easily digestible. In Africa, the green leaves of the cassava plant are also popular as a cooked vegetable and are added to soups and stews.

**Eggplant (garden egg):** In Ghana, garden eggs are small fruits, the size and shape of eggs, and are usually a creamy white to yellow in color. Like tomatoes, garden eggs are treated like a vegetable. They are often dropped into soup to boil and soften, then the skin is slipped off and the vegetable is ground.

Sometimes the garden egg is diced and added to stews. Small Japanese eggplants look more similar to African garden eggs, but the large purple-skinned eggplants sold in grocery stores work fine as a substitute.

**Gari (also known as gali or garri):** This is cassava that has been processed by peeling, slicing, and sun-drying; then grinding or grating it into a coarse flour. Gari is very different from tapioca starch. In Ghana and other parts of West Africa, gari serves as an African convenience food—especially popular with students in boarding schools. It is often mixed with just enough hot water to make it swell up, then served with a hot pepper sauce or stew. It is also eaten as a porridge for breakfast.

**Ginger or ginger root:** Fresh ginger is a knobby root that has a sharp sweet taste. The outside peel is light brown or tan, and the inside is pale yellow. In the United States, we often use dried ground ginger root to flavor gingerbread and pumpkin pies. In Africa, the fresh roots are used in homemade soft drinks, snacks, and main dishes (See the recipes for *Ginger Beer, Akla, Chichinga,* and *Jollof Rice.*)

**Greens:** It has been documented that people in Ghana eat forty-seven different kinds of leafy green vegetables. (That reminds me of when I moved to Pennsylvania and discovered that apples were not just red or yellow—they ranged from golden delicious to Granny Smith to Macintosh to Rome to Ida Red, and so forth.) The greens are usually not eaten raw, but they are cooked in a soup, stew, or side dish along with fish or meat or onions and pepper (see the recipe for *Palaver Sauce*). Some common greens in West Africa include young tender leaves of cassava, cocoyam (*nkontommire*), okra, cowpeas, garden eggs, or sweet potatoes, as well as those greens with names like *efan, akatewa* (a kind of spinach), or *bowene* (bitterleaf). Fresh or frozen spinach and other greens such as collards, mustard greens, kale, chard, or beet tops make good substitutes.

**Lemongrass:** Lemongrass (*Cymbopogon citratus*) is an herb used in Africa to make tea and flavor some soups. It looks like tall thick grass, it grows easily, and it has a lemony smell to it. One Nigerian cookbook mentions that it is grown in African gardens to discourage snakes and tsetse flies.

**Okra:** Okra is a vegetable with green pods that, when cut, have a slimy look and feel to them. It is often used to thicken soups and stews in West Africa. Native to Africa, okra was introduced into the United States by the enslaved Africans. The word *okra* itself comes from the Twi word *nkuruma*. *Gumbo* is another African word for okra. Frozen okra is readily available in local supermarkets, even when fresh okra is not.

**Palm oil and palmnuts:** Palm oil, which comes from the oil palm tree (*elaeis guineensis*), is a very popular orange-red cooking oil with a distinctive flavor. Rich in vitamin A and highly-saturated, the oil is extracted from the small, round red fruit (the palmnut) by boiling the fruits, then pounding them, and washing and straining the pulp. A form of palm fruit known as palm cream or palm butter is used in soups. Canned cream of palm fruits is exported from both Ghana and the Ivory Coast. Another oil produced from the palm kernels is used in making cosmetics and moisturizing the hair and body. The oil palm tree has many other uses and has been referred to as "probably the most useful tree in West Africa."

**Papaya:** In Ghana and other parts of Africa, the papaya or treemelon is known as *pawpaw*. Many Western cookbooks insist that the name *pawpaw* is incorrect because it is also the name of a North American fruit of similar color that grows wild in the Ozarks, is about half a foot long, and tastes similar to bananas. However, African cookbooks routinely call papaya by its popular African name *pawpaw*, and that is good enough for me. At any rate, this tropical fruit often grows much larger in Ghana than the kind of papaya found in stores in the United States, which are most likely from Hawaii. The outside skin of the pawpaw, or papaya, is green and hard when it is unripe, and blotchy green-yellow and slightly soft when it is ripe. They should not be bruised or too soft when you buy them. The inside is a often a cheerful orange color with soft dark seeds in the center, although other kinds have fruit ranging in color from pink to red. The inside fruit tastes like a cross between a cantaloupe and a peach.

**Plantain:** The big sister of our common banana, plantains are a staple food in many tropical countries. They have a mild flavor, are much starchier and firmer than bananas, and must always be cooked before they are eaten. They may be eaten as a vegetable side dish, a starchy accompaniment to a soup or stew, a snack, a dessert, an entree, or used to flavor and thicken a soup or stew. They are served baked, boiled, fried, mashed, or roasted. They are delicious at any stage of the ripening process—hard and green (wonderful for chips), yellow, or very ripe and soft with black skin. Be warned that sometimes during the winter, imported plantains do not ripen properly and turn hard and woody. If the plantain is yellow or black, but has not softened at all (similar to the way a banana softens), discard it. Also, do not try to ripen them in a cold place like a refrigerator.

**Yam:** In the U.S., we use the word *yam* to refer to something very different from the African yam. By *yam* we usually mean *sweet potato*, which is from a tropical plant (*Ipomoea batatas*) that comes from the morning glory family. Africans eat these sweet potatoes too, but the word Africans use for yam comes from African words like *name* or *nyami*. African yams are from a completely different type of plant of the genus Dioscorea. In other words, the two foods are very different in taste, texture, and appearance. African yams are much more similar to pota-toes than sweet potatoes. Their skin is thicker and more like bark than the skin on a potato; and the flesh is usually white (or sometimes yellow) and firmer than that of potatoes. Yams can weigh as little as a pound, and I am told that they can weigh as much as a hundred pounds! They are important in West African cooking and society, and there are many yam feast days. Like potatoes, yams can be eaten in many different ways—boiled, fried, mashed, or pounded (see the recipes for Fufu and Ampesi).

# Metric Conversion Table

Use this chart to help you change standard U.S. measuring units to their approximate metric equivalents:

| Standard U.S. Unit | Metric Equivalent |
|---|---|
| ⅛ teaspoon | .5 milliliter (ml) |
| ¼ teaspoon | 1 ml |
| ½ teaspoon | 2 ml |
| 1 teaspoon | 5 ml |
| 1 tablespoon (3 teaspoons) | 15 ml |
| ⅛ cup (2 tablespoons) | 30 ml |
| ¼ cup (4 tablespoons) | 50 ml |
| ⅓ cup (5 tablespoons) | 75 ml |
| ½ cup (8 tablespoons) | 125 ml |
| 1 cup (16 tablespoons) | 250 ml |
| 4 cups (1 quart) | 1 liter |
| 1 ounce | 30 grams (g) |
| 1 pound | 500 g |
| 2 pounds | 1 kilogram (kg) |
| ¼ inch | .5 centimeter (cm) |
| ½ inch | 1 cm |
| 1 inch | 2.5 cm |

A GOOD SOUP ATTRACTS CHAIRS

# A GOOD SOUP ATTRACTS CHAIRS

# Drinks

# Lemon Squash

This is a lot like lemonade. It is called "squash" because of all the fruit you squash to make the concentrate that you add water to for the drink. It is handy because you can make it ahead of time and store it in the refrigerator for thirsty summer days or when a friend drops by for a visit.

**INGREDIENTS:**
- 1 cup water
- 1 cup sugar
- 5 large lemons (or enough to get 1 cup of juice)

**UTENSILS:**
- spoon
- knife for cutting lemons
- cutting board
- watch or timer
- small pitcher or quart jar
- 1-cup measuring cup
- 3-quart saucepan
- small bowl
- wooden spoon for stirring

**DIRECTIONS:**
1. Assemble the ingredients and utensils.
2. Wash the lemons with water.
3. Roll the lemons on a countertop to make them easy to squeeze.
4. Cut the lemons in half on the cutting board.
5. Use the juicer to squeeze the lemons to get about 1 cup of juice. Pour the juice into a bowl. Use the spoon to remove any seeds that may have fallen in with the juice.
6. Put the cup of water and cup of sugar into the small pan.
7. Hold the handle of the pan and stir the water and sugar mixture over medium heat until the sugar is completely dissolved. It will take about 5 minutes.

8. Turn the heat to medium-high and carefully pour in the juice. Keep stirring and boil the mixture for 2 minutes.
9. Turn off the heat and remove the mixture from the stove. Let it cool a little, then pour it carefully into a small pitcher or jar.
10. When the squash is cool, cover it and store it in the refrigerator.

## TO SERVE:

Shake or stir the squash mixture, and pour about ¼ cup of it into each glass. Add about ¼ cup of water to each, and stir. Taste the squash. If it is too sweet, add a little more water.

## VARIATIONS:

1. For fun or a party, add ice cubes to the glass and use ¼ cup soda water (instead of the regular water) with the ¼ cup squash. Add more water or squash if you want, and dress up the glass with a little slice of lime, lemon, or orange).
2. There are lots of other fruits that Africans use to make squashes. Two common ones are limes and oranges. To make *Lime Squash*, just use limes instead of lemons in the recipe. If the limes are small, it may take up to 8 of them to get a cup of juice. Limes are a little sweeter than lemons, so the squash has a different flavor. To make *Orange Squash*, you need more oranges and less water and sugar. Use ¾ cup sugar, ¾ cup water, and 8 oranges (about 1¾ to 2 cups of orange juice) to make the squash; then serve it the same way you serve the other squashes.
3. Also, if you don't want to store the squash, and you plan to drink it right away, there is really no need to cook it first—just squash and serve!

*Lemon Squash*

*Ginger Beer*

# Ginger Beer

This homemade soft drink can be found in all parts of sub-Saharan Africa. It does take patience and planning, but it keeps well and can be made ahead for a party. Americans in the southern United States may have already heard of ginger beer. I found one recipe with identical ingredients and only slight changes in directions in a Creole cookbook published in New Orleans in 1901 and another in a recent African cookbook.

**INGREDIENTS:**

3 ounces fresh ginger root
2 cups boiling water
2 cups cold water
½ cup sugar
½ lime (or lemon) (to get 2 tablespoons juice)
6 whole cloves
¼ stick cinnamon (about ¼ inch)

**UTENSILS:**

vegetable peeler
paring knife
grater
2-quart casserole dish or other large glass bowl (We use a casserole dish because it has a flat bottom that won't tip over easily.)
1-cup measuring cup
1-quart saucepan (to boil water)
dish towel or bath towel (folded)
potato masher or wooden spoon
cheesecloth
strainer or colander
glass bowl
cutting board
1-teaspoon measuring spoon
pitcher

## DIRECTIONS:

1. Assemble ingredients and utensils.
2. Rinse the fresh ginger with cold water.
3. Using a vegetable peeler or paring knife, carefully scrape off the thin peeling of the ginger.
4. Grate the ginger into the casserole dish.
5. Put 2 cups of water into a saucepan, then put it on the stove over high heat to bring it to a boil.
6. While waiting for the water to boil, set the casserole dish on top of the folded towel to keep it from sliding around; then pound and bruise the ginger well with a potato masher or wooden spoon.
7. After you have mashed the ginger well, carefully pour the boiling water over it. (Be sure to turn off the burner on the stove.)
8. Let the ginger-water mixture sit for at least 2 hours.
9. After 2 hours, fold the cheesecloth several times and line the strainer or colander with it. Place the strainer or colander over another glass bowl. Carefully pour the ginger-water mixture through the cheesecloth to strain it into the bowl. Squeeze, twist, and press the cloth to get most of the liquid from the ginger pulp.
10. To the liquid in the bowl, add 2 cups of cold water and ½ cup to ¾ cup sugar. Stir well to dissolve the sugar.
11. Wash the lime (or lemon). Roll it on a table or countertop to make it juicy, pressing down while you roll it back and forth. Cut it in half with a knife on the cutting board, then squeeze the juice from one half into a cup. Use a spoon to press the inside of the lime to help get the juice out. You should have about 2 tablespoons of juice. Take out any seeds, then pour the juice into the ginger-water mixture. Add the cloves and cinnamon and let it sit for at least an hour.
12. After an hour, remove the cloves and cinnamon with a spoon.
13. Carefully pour the ginger beer into a pitcher, leaving most of the white sediment in the bottom of the bowl. Store the covered pitcher in the refrigerator.

**TO SERVE:**

Drink the ginger beer over ice cubes and mixed with water, ginger ale, or seltzer water. Use about ½ cup of each for one generous serving.

**VARIATIONS:**

There are many different ways to make ginger beer. Sometimes it has more or less ginger, sometimes it is made with pineapple instead of lemon or lime. Some people make it with yeast and cream of tartar. Some people like to add the whole cloves and stick cinnamon to flavor it, some do not. Some people drink it chilled over ice, others like to add water or ginger ale or club soda to it. Any way you make it, it is a great drink for a thirsty day.

# Orange Juice

The smell and taste of fresh orange juice makes me think of travelling in Ghana. Young girls or women often have neat piles of oranges for sale at bus stops or at convenient places around town. When a customer arrives, they quickly cut off a thin layer of peel all around the orange, then cut off the top; and the buyer walks or rides away squeezing the orange and sucking the juice. It really quenches your thirst, and there is no need for a glass!

Freshly-squeezed orange juice is a readily available beverage too. Most of us are used to orange juice from cans or bottles or cartons. It is amazing how delicious fresh juice is when you make it yourself—and it is not hard either. To make enough juice for one person, use two large (or three small) oranges. We like to use California navel oranges, which don't have any seeds, and we find that two oranges usually make about one-half cup of juice.

*Orange Juice*

## INGREDIENTS:
  **2 oranges per person**

## UTENSILS:
  **knife**
  **cutting board**
  **plastic, glass, or metal juicer**
  **glass or pitcher**

## DIRECTIONS:
1.  Assemble the ingredients and utensils.
2.  Wash the oranges.
3.  Cut them in half on the cutting board.
4.  If you have a juicer with a strainer and a glass cup attached, just put the cut side of the orange onto the juicer and push down on the orange half while you squeeze and turn it back and forth until most of the juice is out. Do the same thing with the other three orange halves. Pour the juice into a glass, and it is ready to drink. (If you have a

juicer without a glass container attached, just set the juicer on top of a bowl or glass to catch the juice before you start squeezing the orange.)
5. If you are making juice for your whole family or several friends, you will need to pour the juice from the glass or bowl into a pitcher as you make it.

**TO SERVE:**

Of course, freshly squeezed orange juice doesn't really need any decorating. It looks great by itself, but for extra special times, I cut a thin slice of lime and cut it a little to put it on the side of the juice glasses (see the photograph).

**VARIATIONS:**

You can strain the orange juice if you prefer it without the pulp. If the oranges are not sweet, add a little sugar to the juice.

*Lemongrass Tea*

# Lemongrass Tea

It was not until several years after we were married that I first tasted lemongrass tea. When my husband smelled it brewing, he was carried right back to his childhood. He said, "My mother always had lemongrass growing in the garden for tea. It was so good with milk and sugar."

Lemongrass is an herb that is easy to grow indoors in a sunny windowbox, or outdoors during warm weather. If you don't have fresh lemongrass near you, dried lemongrass is usually carried by natural food stores or tea shops. This soothing tea is wonderful for a mid-morning or afternoon snack—especially when accompanied by *Twisted Cakes* or *African Doughnuts*.

**INGREDIENTS:**

>  fresh or dried lemongrass
>  water
>  1 small can evaporated milk
>  sugar

**UTENSILS:**

>  mugs or teapot
>  saucepan, microwave-safe pitcher, electric tea kettle,
>    or hot pot
>  tea strainer or teaball
>  teaspoon
>  measuring cup
>  can opener
>  milk pitcher
>  sugar bowl

**DIRECTIONS:**

A single cup of tea is easy to make in a microwave oven:

1.  Fill a microwave-safe mug two-thirds full with water. Heat for about 2 minutes, or just until boiling, in the microwave.

2. There are tea strainers that work like recyclable teabags made especially for single servings of loose tea. If you have one of these, fill it with a teaspoon of dried lemongrass, and set it into the hot water to steep for about 5 minutes. (The tea leaves will soak up some of the water, so do not fill the tea strainer too full.) If you have no special strainer, pour one heaping teaspoon of dried lemongrass directly into each cup. If you are using fresh lemongrass, wash the lemongrass in cold water, cut it into 1-inch pieces, then pour ½ cup of the loose lemongrass into each cup.
3. While the tea is steeping, or brewing, shake the can of evaporated milk well, then open it with the can opener and pour the milk into a small pitcher.
4. After about 5 minutes, hold the tea strainer over another cup and carefully pour the tea into the cup, straining out the tea leaves.

This tea is so good that you would probably rather make a whole teapot, so you can have seconds and share it with friends:

1. First, fill the teapot with hot water from the tap and let it sit to warm the pot while you prepare everything else.
2. Heat 4 cups of water to a boil. We use an electric kettle or hot pot, but you can also use a saucepan on the stove or pitcher in a microwave oven.
3. While the water is heating, shake the evaporated milk well, then open it with the can opener and pour it into the milk pitcher.
4. If you are using fresh lemongrass, rinse it with cold water and cut it into one-inch pieces. Without packing down the leaves, measure out 2 cups of fresh lemongrass. If you are using dried lemongrass, measure out 4 heaping teaspoons of it.
5. When the water boils, unplug the electric tea kettle or hot pot, or turn off the heat on the stove.

6. Empty the hot tap water from the teapot.
7. Put the washed fresh lemongrass leaves or dried lemongrass into the teapot, pour the boiling water over it, then put the lid on the teapot.
8. After 5 minutes, stir the tea once with a spoon. If you like, hold a tea strainer over the cups to keep the tea leaves out as you pour the tea.

**TO SERVE:**

Stir in 1 or 2 teaspoons of sugar and some evaporated milk (we like a couple of tablespoons per mug of tea). It is delicious!

**VARIATIONS:**

There are several variations on this tea recipe. You can leave out the milk or sugar, or use honey instead of sugar. You could use herbal tea in a teabag—many lemon herb teas have lemongrass in them. You could also use regular tea in teabags and enjoy it the same way. In Ghana, people sometimes use the word *tea* to mean almost any hot drink—including regular tea, herb teas, coffee, or hot chocolate.

You could use regular milk if you do not have evaporated milk; but in much of West Africa—where the tsetse fly has made cattle-breeding very difficult for many years and many people do not have refrigerators—canned, or tinned, milk is preferred. It is richer than regular milk, and it tastes creamier.

# Main Courses

# Peanut Butter Stew or Soup with Chicken

*Peanut Butter Stew* is called "groundnut stew" in Ghana, where peanuts are known as groundnuts. It is creamy and yummy and fun to serve at dinner parties. Peanut Butter Soup is called *Nkate Nkwan* in the Twi language (*nkate* means "groundnut" or "peanut," and *nkwan* means "soup"). The only difference between the soup and the stew is the amount of water you add. For stew, you add only three cups of water, and for soup you add six cups of water.

## INGREDIENTS:
   3 to 4 pounds chicken pieces
   2 medium onions
   3 or 6 cups water
   1½ teaspoons salt
   ½ to 1 cup creamy peanut butter (natural-style with no sugar added)
   1 8-ounce can tomato sauce
   ⅛ teaspoon ground red pepper (more or less to taste)

Note: If you are serving peanut butter stew with condiments (see serving directions), you will need an assortment of ingredients (like green peppers, coconut, bananas, tomatoes, peanuts, etc.) to chop and put into bowls.

## UTENSILS:
   large soup pot (5-quart or larger)
   cutting knife
   cutting board
   1-cup measuring cup
   measuring spoons (⅛, ½ and 1 teaspoon)
   can opener
   wooden spoon
   small 1-quart saucepan
   soup ladle

**DIRECTIONS:**

1. Pull or cut off most of the skin from the chicken pieces, rinse the chicken with water, then put the pieces into a soup pot. (The chicken skins may be left on, but a better flavor and less oil is obtained by removing them first.)

2. Peel and chop the onions on the cutting board, then add them along with 3 cups (for stew) or 6 cups (for soup) of water and the salt to the pot with the chicken.

3. Put the pot on the stove and turn the burner to high. When the water boils, turn the heat to low and cover the pot.

4. Open the can of tomato sauce with the can opener and add the sauce to the soup. Stir with a wooden spoon to mix.

5. Put the peanut butter in a medium saucepan. Carefully ladle about 2 cups of the soup broth into the saucepan. Slowly stir the broth and peanut butter mixture until it is creamy.

6. Now, slowly stir the peanut butter mixture into the soup, being careful not to splatter.

7. Add the red pepper, stir again, and cover the pot. Let it cook gently on low for about half an hour. Add a little more water if necessary.

**TO SERVE:**

Peanut Butter Stew is tasty simply spooned on top of plain boiled rice. However, for a party, it is great to serve the stew with rice and condiments, like curry. Just chop several toppings, like chopped peanuts (unsalted), bananas, oranges, tomatoes, green peppers, coconut, hard-boiled egg, onions, or whatever you like; and put them in small bowls. Put a spoonful of boiled white rice on a plate, cover it with some of the stew, and add your choice of toppings. This recipe will easily serve four to six people. Peanut butter soup goes well with *Rice Balls* or *Fufu*.

**VARIATIONS:**

1. Add ½ package (5 ounces) of frozen chopped okra to the soup when you add the red pepper.

2. Substitute ⅓ cup dried minced onions for the fresh onions.
3. Substitute a 6-ounce can of tomato paste for the tomato sauce.
4. Add one or two teaspoons of instant chicken bouillon and use only ½ teaspoon salt.
5. Use chunky instead of creamy-style peanut butter.

*Peanut Butter Stew with Chicken*

# Jollof Rice

This dish is bright orange-red in color, which makes it look similar to Spanish rice. It was probably introduced by the Jollof (or Wolof) tribe from Gambia, but it is now popular throughout West Africa and beyond. It is a delicious one-pot meal that can also be made ahead of time and reheated. Jollof rice can be made with chicken, beef, or seafood, and has many variations. The following recipe is our family's favorite version.

## INGREDIENTS:

- 3 teaspoons salt
- ⅛ teaspoon ground red pepper
- ½ teaspoon garlic powder
- 1 teaspoon curry powder
- ¼ teaspoon ground dried ginger
- 1 large onion
- 1 small roasting chicken (or 3 pounds chicken parts or boneless chicken)
- 1 tablespoon peanut oil (or other vegetable oil)
- 2 cups long-grain rice (not instant)
- 3 cups water
- 1 6-ounce can tomato paste
- 1 16-ounce can tomatoes
- 1 10-ounce package peas and carrots (frozen)

## UTENSILS:

small bowl
measuring spoons
cutting board
knives (paring and butcher)
10-inch frying pan
wooden spoon
pancake turner
large bowl
dutch oven (large pot) with lid
measuring cup
can opener
small saucepan with lid

**DIRECTIONS:**

1. Assemble the ingredients and utensils.
2. In a small bowl, mix together 1 teaspoon of the salt with the red pepper, garlic powder, curry powder, and ginger. Set aside.
3. Chop the onion on the cutting board, then set it aside. (It helps to keep onion in the refrigerator before cutting it— then it doesn't sting your eyes as much.)
4. Rinse the chicken and remove as much skin and fat as possible. Wipe it dry with a paper towel or cloth.
5. Cut the chicken into bite-sized pieces. Get a grown-up or a butcher to help with this because whacking the bones to break through them can be dangerous. You should get about 20 or 30 pieces.
6. Heat the tablespoon of oil in the frying pan over medium heat. Brown the chicken a few pieces at a time, pushing the

*Jollof Rice*

almost-browned ones to one side of the pan as you cook them.

7. While the chicken pieces are browning, sprinkle them with the spice mixture. Stir the chicken pieces with a spatula or wooden spoon to coat them all. Keep turning the pieces, and remove the browned ones to a large bowl to make room for the rest. Tongs help when removing the browned pieces. Be careful of splattering oil when placing the chicken into the hot oil and when removing it.

8. Fry the chopped onions in the same frying pan over medium heat for about 2 minutes. When they start to look clear (or translucent), add the two cups of rice to the onions. Stir the rice and onions well to mix them together. Be careful not to burn the rice. Scrape the pan well while you stir, and turn the heat to low.

9. Remove the frying pan from the heat and turn the stove off.

10. Carefully pour the rice and onions from the frying pan into the large pot or dutch oven. Add one cup of water to the pan to help rinse out the onion, then add that to the pot.

11. Open the cans of tomato paste and tomatoes, and add both to the large pot. Smash the tomatoes against the side of the pan with a wooden spoon, or squeeze them through your fingers as you add them to the pot, so they fall apart.

12. Add 2 teaspoons salt and 2 cups of water, and stir well. Add the chicken pieces and juices from the large bowl, then stir again.

13. Bring the mixture to a boil over medium high heat, cover, turn the heat to low, and simmer gently until the rice is tender, about 20 minutes. Check after about 10 minutes and stir gently to make sure the rice at the bottom of the pan is not burning or scorching. If you think it might be, add a little more water (about ½ cup). When the rice is just tender (soft), turn off the heat and leave the pan tightly covered to rest for about 20 more minutes.

**TO SERVE:**

Cook frozen peas and carrots in a half cup of boiling water in a small saucepan. They will only take a few minutes to cook. Turn down the heat to low after the water boils, and cover the pan, so the water doesn't all boil away. When the rice is cooked, stir half of the peas and carrots into the rice, and sprinkle half on top just before serving. We like to serve Jollof Rice and a crisp green salad for a delicious dinner. It also goes well with a cooked vegetable as a side dish.

**VARIATIONS:**

1.  Substitute 1½ pounds of beef cut into small cubes for the chicken.
2.  Add ½ cup of washed and deveined fresh or frozen shrimp to the chicken or beef version after you add the water and rice. Omit the peas and carrots.
3.  Use a tablespoon or two of dried shrimp instead of fresh or frozen shrimp.

# Palaver Sauce

In Ghana, when people talk about a *palaver*, they mean there has been some kind of trouble; and it usually takes a lot of talking to sort out and solve the problem. Perhaps the name of this sauce came to Ghana from the Portuguese, who were early colonists in Ghana whose word for "word" is *palavra*. At any rate, palaver sauce ingredients, which you might expect to get into trouble with each other (like beef and fish), simmer quite well together. There are many different versions of this stew found throughout West Africa, but the use of greens is common to them all.

## INGREDIENTS:

½ pound stewing beef
salt (the amount will depend on how salty your fish
   or ham cubes are—it will probably be about ½
   to 1 teaspoon)
2 cups water
1 medium onion, chopped
¼ cup palm oil (or peanut or other vegetable oil)
½ pound frozen fish fillets (cod or haddock)
1 10-ounce package frozen chopped spinach
1 10-ounce package frozen collard greens
1 16-ounce can tomatoes
¼ teaspoon ground red pepper (or more to taste)
½ cup ground agushi
½ pound smoked whiting (or smoked ham cubes or
   2 tablespoons dried shrimp)

## UTENSILS:

knife
cutting board
5-quart soup pot
measuring cups
wooden spoon
can opener
measuring spoons
fork
small bowl

## DIRECTIONS:

1.  Assemble the ingredients and utensils.
2.  Cut the meat into ½-inch cubes and put them into the pot
    with the salt and 2 cups of water (if you are using ham
    cubes, you can add them too). Set the soup pot on the
    stove over high heat, stir it, and bring the water to a boil.
    Cover the pot, reduce the heat to medium, and allow the
    meat to simmer.

3. Peel and chop the onion, then add it and the oil to the pot on the stove. Add the frozen fish, whole or in pieces, to the pot. Next add the spinach and collard greens to the pot and turn the heat up to high. When the ingredients come to a boil, lower the heat to medium, cover the pan, and continue cooking the sauce.

4. Open the can of tomatoes and add them to the pot, smashing them against the side of the soup pot until they fall apart or breaking them up with your fingers in a small bowl first, then adding them.

5. Add the ¼ teaspoon red pepper and stir the sauce well.

6. Now it is time to thicken the sauce. Mix the agushi in a small bowl with about ½ cup of liquid from the pot, then stir the agushi mixture into the pot with the sauce.

7. While the sauce cooks down and thickens, prepare the smoked fish (unless you are using the smoked ham). Rinse the fish, remove any skin or bones, and break it to pieces. This takes some practice. Gently stir the fish into the sauce.

8. Simmer the sauce, uncovered, on low heat until most of the liquid is gone and the meat is tender. Stir it every once in a while.

*Palaver Sauce*

**TO SERVE:**

Palaver sauce is good with boiled potatoes or boiled rice.

**VARIATIONS:**

1. If you don't have fresh onion, use frozen or dried minced onion.
2. Instead of a 16-ounce can of tomatoes, use 3 fresh tomatoes or a 6-ounce can of tomato paste and ½ cup of water.
3. Use ½ cup oil instead of ¼ cup.
4. There are various other thickeners that you can substitute for the agushi. You can use 2 eggs: Break them into a small bowl and beat them with a fork. Use a cup to dip out about ½ cup of liquid from the pot and add it to the eggs. Mix this with the fork, then pour it into the sauce, and stir.

    You can use 1 cup of Mexican refried beans or cooked, mashed red beans. Just stir them into the cooking liquid before adding it to the pot.

    You can peel 1 small eggplant, boil it until it is soft, then grind it in a blender with one egg. Stir the mixture into the sauce and watch it thicken.

# Palmnut Soup

When we were newly married, my husband told me that his mother always made two big pots of soup on New Year's Day. One pot was palmnut soup, or *abɛ (pronounced ah-*beh) *nkwan* (*nkwan* is "soup" in the Twi language, and *abɛ* are the red palmnuts); and the other pot was groundnut soup, or *nkate nkwan* (*nkate* is groundnut or peanut, and *nkwan* is soup). We have carried on that tradition in our family, and every New Year's Day we try to invite other Africans living in our town to come and celebrate with us. On New Year's Day, we make a somewhat fancy version of palmnut soup. This recipe makes a large pot for a party that will serve ten to twelve people, or more if there are other dishes as well.

There is no subsitute for the cream of palmnuts in this recipe. To find it you have to go to a store that specializes in African foods. If you cannot find canned cream of palmnuts, make *Light Soup* or *Peanut Butter Soup* instead. If you find it, make this soup because the rich red creamy taste is not only unique, but it tastes good, too. Watch out for spills because the red palm oil makes stains that won't wash out easily!

**INGREDIENTS:**

- 2 large onions
- 2 pounds beef (bottom round roast, stewing beef or chuck roast)
- water
- 2 teaspoons salt
- 2 pounds beef soup bones
- 1 eggplant (3 cups chopped)
- 1 28-ounce can of pureed tomatoes
- 1 29-ounce can cream of palmnuts
- 1 pound fresh mushrooms
- 6 ounces smoked fish (white fish, whiting, or salmon)
- ½ pound fresh shrimp (with shells)
- 3 small crabs
- ¼ to ½ teaspoon dried ground red pepper
- 1 10-ounce package frozen chopped okra

**UTENSILS:**

- knife for chopping
- cutting board
- large (8-quart) soup pot with lid
- measuring cup
- 2-quart saucepan with lid
- timer
- can opener
- paper towels
- electric blender (or food processor)
- measuring spoons
- wooden spoon
- soup ladle

**DIRECTIONS:**

1. Assemble ingredients and utensils.
2. Peel and chop the 2 onions and put them into a large, heavy soup pot.
3. Cut off the fat and gristle, then cut the beef into ½-inch cubes. Add the beef cubes, enough water to cover them (about 4 to 6 cups), and 2 teaspoons salt to the pot.
4. Add the soup bones, cover the pot, and bring the water to a boil over high heat. When the water boils, turn it to low, and allow it to simmer while you prepare the eggplant.
5. Rinse the eggplant under cold water. Cut off the ends and cut it in half. Use a knife to cut off the purple skin, then cut the eggplant into ½-inch cubes until you have about 3 cups. Put the eggplant into the 2-quart saucepan with 3 cups of water. Cover the saucepan and put it on the stove on high heat. When the water boils, turn the heat down to low and allow it to simmer for 10 minutes (use a timer so you don't forget about it). Remove from heat.
6. Open the can of tomato puree and add it to the soup pot.
7. Open the can of cream of palmnuts and pour it into the pot. Allow the soup to simmer for 30 minutes while you prepare the other ingredients.
8. Rinse the mushrooms quickly under cold water and wipe them clean and dry with paper towels. Trim the ends off of the stems, but don't cut the whole stem off. Cut the mushrooms in half.
9. Remove the skin and bones from the smoked fish. Throw away the skin and bones.
10. Rinse the shrimp and crabs under cold water.
11. Using an electric blender (or food processor), puree about half of the eggplant and water mixture and pour it into the soup pot. Puree the other half of the eggplant and water mixture and add it too.
12. Add the mushrooms, smoked fish, shrimp, crabs, frozen okra, and ¼ to ½ teaspoon of ground red pepper. Stir the soup with a wooden spoon.

13. Cover the soup pot again and allow it to cook on low for 20 minutes, or until the meat and vegetables are soft and the flavors have blended together. I usually use a spoon to skim off the palm oil that rises to the top (save it in a jar to use when cooking stews). Just before serving, taste the soup and add more salt and red pepper if necessary.

**TO SERVE:**

This does make a big pot of soup, and we often just serve it from the pot on a counter, buffet-style, with platters of rice balls and fufu next to it. Of course, you could also ladle it into a serving bowl or soup tureen, and serve it at the table. It also reheats nicely if made the day before.

**VARIATIONS:**

1. Leave out any or all of the extras—shrimp, crabs, smoked fish, eggplant, mushrooms, soup bones, or okra—but be sure to include the cream of palmnuts, beef, onions, tomatoes, peppers, and salt.

2. Leave the eggplant in cubes, and add it and the water you cook it in without pureeing it.
3. Use fresh or canned tomatoes or tomato paste in place of the canned pureed tomatoes.
4. Use fresh okra instead of frozen okra.
5. Use goat meat instead of beef.
6. To prepare a smaller version of the soup that will fit in a 5-quart soup pot, buy an 18-ounce can of cream of palmnuts, and cut the rest of the recipe in half.

# Light Soup

Light soup (also known as "pepper soup" or *nkrakra*) is the first African soup that I learned to make. My husband's younger sister Eunice, or Afua, taught me how to cook it. Afua was her *day name*, meaning she was a girl born on a Friday; and her family and close friends called her by that rather than her Christian name, Eunice.

*Light Soup*

My husband's (and Afua's) mother died when he was only twelve years old, but she was a very intelligent and remarkable woman. In her day, girls were not supposed to be educated, so she ran away from home to go to school. She studied domestic science, went on to attend teacher training college, and became a very respected family and community leader. She believed that both her sons and her daughters should be educated in everything, and I'll always be grateful to her for teaching her oldest son to sew and cook. Everyone was proud of her and in awe of her industriousness. Among other things, she kept goats; and if she were making this soup for a special occasion, it might include goat meat instead of beef. If she had gotten some "grasscutter" meat from a hunter, she might have prepared it with that instead.

It is a simple and satisfying soup. In Ghana, it would probably be peppery enough to make your nose run while you ate it, but it is fine to make this milder version too.

## INGREDIENTS:
- **1 pound stewing beef**
- **1 large onion**
- **1¼ teaspoons salt**
- **6 cups plus 1½ cups water**
- **1 small eggplant (about 2 or 3 cups, cubed)**
- **1 16-ounce can tomatoes**
- **½ pound smoked whiting**
- **⅛ to ¼ teaspoon ground red pepper (or more to taste)**

## UTENSILS:
- **cutting board**
- **knife**
- **5-quart soup pot and cover**
- **1-cup measuring cup**
- **small saucepan with cover**
- **timer**
- **can opener**
- **electric blender**
- **slotted spoon**
- **measuring spoons**

**DIRECTIONS:**
1. Assemble ingredients and utensils.
2. Cut the meat into one-inch cubes on the cutting board, then put them into a large pot.
3. Peel and chop the onion and add it to the pot.
4. Add 6 cups of water and 1¼ teaspoons (or 1 heaping teaspoon) of salt to the pot.
5. Bring the water, meat, onion, and salt to a boil on high heat, then turn the heat to low. Cover the pot and let the meat simmer for 45 minutes, or until it is almost tender. Check once or twice to make sure the meat is still covered with water.
6. While the meat simmers, rinse and peel the eggplant and cut it into chunks.
7. Put the chunks into a small saucepan, along with 1½ cups of water.
8. Bring the water and eggplant cubes to a boil over high heat. Reduce the heat to low, partly cover the pan, and simmer the eggplant for 10 minutes (use a timer if you have one).
9. While the eggplant cooks, open the can of tomatoes and empty it into the blender container.
10. When the eggplant is soft, take the pan off the stove and turn off the heat. Use a slotted spoon (if you have one) to lift the eggplant chunks out of the pan and add them to the tomatoes in the blender container. Do not fill it more than half full. Do the blending in two batches if you need to. Put the blender cover on tightly and blend the eggplant and tomatoes together for 1 minute on low speed.
11. Carefully pour the mixture into the soup pot with the meat. Use the eggplant liquid in the pan to rinse out the rest of the tomato eggplant mixture in the blender, then add it to the soup.

12. Remove the skin and bones from the fish (younger cooks should ask a grown-up to help them), and add the fish and ⅛ teaspoon of red pepper to the soup. Allow the soup to simmer for 20 minutes. Taste the soup to see if it needs any more salt or red pepper.

**TO SERVE:**

In Ghana, light soup is often eaten with fufu. It is also good with a thick slice of crusty French bread or pita bread warmed for a minute in the microwave.

**VARIATIONS:**
1. Leave out the smoked fish or use smoked ham cubes instead of smoked fish.
2. Use goat meat, pork, or chicken instead of beef.
3. Leave out the eggplant.
4. Use a small can of tomato paste and 2 cups of water instead of the tomatoes; or use a large can of tomato sauce instead of tomatoes; or grind 4 large fresh tomatoes instead of canned tomatoes.
5. Substitute zucchini for the eggplant.
6. Make a vegetarian version, using a mixture of eggplant, mushrooms, zucchini, onions, pepper, eggs, and tomatoes; and leave out the meat and fish.

# Vegetarian Groundnut Soup

My husband's father, like many Africans, was a vegetarian. He knew what we in the United States have only recently been learning—eating well doesn't have to mean eating meat. This creamy vegetarian soup uses five kinds of vegetables, peanuts, and eggs to make a hearty soup that goes well with *Fufu* or *Rice Balls*. Our children like it with thick slices of crusty French bread to dunk in it. This recipe serves six people. We like to top it off with *Tropical Fruit Salad* for dessert.

## INGREDIENTS:

6 eggs
water
½ teaspoon salt
1 small eggplant (3 cups chopped)
1 large onion (1 cup chopped)
1½ teaspoons salt
1 cup canned pureed tomatoes
1 cup creamy peanut butter (natural-style with no
   sugar added)
¼ teaspoon ground red pepper
½ pound large mushrooms (8 ounces)
½ of a 10-ounce package sliced frozen okra
   (5 ounces)

## UTENSILS:

1-quart saucepan
measuring spoons (¼ teaspoon, ½ teaspoon,
   1 teaspoon)
timer
slotted spoon
1-cup measuring cup
knife
2-quart saucepan with lid
cutting board
5-quart soup pot with lid
electric blender (or food processor)
can opener
wooden spoon
soup ladle
paper towel

## DIRECTIONS:

1.  Assemble ingredients and utensils.
2.  To hard boil the eggs, put them in a small, 1-quart sauce-pan and cover them with water. Add ½ teaspoon salt and set the pan on the stove on medium high heat. Bring it to a boil and cook for 10 minutes. Use a slotted spoon to remove the eggs to cool (or carry the pan to the sink, pour

off the hot water, and fill the pan with cold water to let the eggs cool in the pan). When they are cool, peel them.

3. While the eggs are boiling and cooling, prepare the soup. First, rinse the eggplant under cold water. Use a knife to cut off the ends, cut it in half, and cut off the purple skin. On the cutting board, cut the peeled eggplant into ½-inch cubes until you have 3 cups.

4. Put the 3 cups of eggplant into the 2-quart saucepan with 3 cups of water. Cover the saucepan and put it on the stove on high heat. When the water boils, turn the heat down to low, and simmer for 10 minutes.

5. While the eggplant cooks, peel the onion and chop it finely on the cutting board. Put 1 cup of the chopped onion and 4 cups of water into a 5-quart soup pot.

6. Using an electric blender (or food processor) puree about half of the eggplant and water mixture, then pour it into the soup pot with the onion and water. Blend the other half of the eggplant and water mixture and add it too.

7. Add 1 ½ teaspoons of salt to the onion, water, and egg-plant broth. Open the can of tomato puree and add 1 cup of the puree to the soup. Turn the heat to high and bring

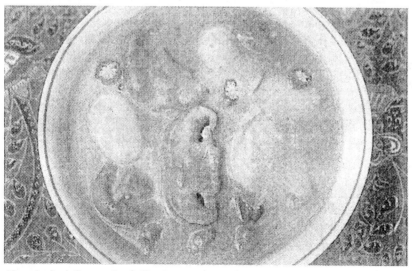

*Vegetarian Groundnut Soup*

the mixture to a boil. When the broth boils, turn the heat down to low and let it simmer, covered, while you prepare the peanut butter. If you like, you can use a spoon to skim the foam off the top of the soup and discard it.

8. To prepare the peanut butter, put 1 cup of creamy peanut butter into the saucepan that you used to cook the eggplant. Add 1 cup of water and stir the peanut butter and water into a smooth paste. Set the pan on the stove on medium heat, and stir until the peanut butter paste is almost boiling. You must stir constantly to keep the peanut butter from scorching. To prevent splattering, remove the pan from the heat just before the mixture comes to a boil. Mix 1 cup of the soup broth in with the peanut butter mixture. Now you can slowly pour the peanut butter mixture from the saucepan into the soup pot, and stir it all together. If you stir the peanut butter right into the soup mixture, it "curdles" and it doesn't mix together to make a creamy soup.

9. Add ¼ teaspoon of ground red pepper.

10. Quickly rinse the mushrooms under cold water and dry them with a paper towel. Slice off the ends of the stems (but not the whole stems), and cut the mushrooms in half. Add them to the soup.

11. Open the package of frozen okra, and run it under cool water just until it softens enough to break off half—about 5 ounces—of the okra. Add half to the soup and wrap up the other half and return it to the freezer.

12. Cover the soup and let it simmer for 20 minutes, or until the vegetables are cooked. If you have not yet peeled the eggs, do it while the soup simmers. Cut the peeled eggs in half and add them to the soup just before serving.

**TO SERVE:**

For family meals, we usually carry the soup pot right to the table and ladle the soup directly into our bowls. You could pour it into a soup tureen or a large serving bowl. As I mentioned before, we like this with *Fufu, Rice Balls,* or American-style with thick slices of crusty sourdough French bread.

**VARIATIONS:**

1. Leave the eggs out and serve the soup as the first course of a larger meal.
2. Leave the eggplant in cubes and do not puree it, or puree only half of it.
3. Use fresh tomatoes or a small can of tomato sauce or tomato paste instead of the canned pureed tomatoes.
4. Use fresh okra instead of frozen.
5. Use zucchini squash instead of eggplant.
6. Omit the dried red pepper. Instead, wash and puree fresh hot chili or jalapeno peppers (seeds and all) when you blend the eggplant. Size and hotness of peppers vary greatly, so begin with about a ½-inch length of pepper, and see if that is enough spice for you.

# Gari Foto

This is an African version of fried rice. It uses cassava that has been made into gari instead of rice.

**INGREDIENTS:**

**1 large onion**
**2 large fresh tomatoes (or 3 drained canned tomatoes)**
**½ tin (about 6 oz.) corned beef (or 1 cup leftover fish, meat, or beans)**
**1 tablespoon tomato sauce**
**6 tablespoons peanut oil**
**2 eggs**
**2 cups gari**
**¾ cup water**
**¼ teaspoon salt**
**2 tablespoons red palm oil**
**½ teaspoon ground ginger**
**¼ teaspoon ground red pepper**
**fresh parsley (for garnish)**

**UTENSILS:**

    **knife (for chopping)**
    **cutting board**
    **can opener**
    **2 small mixing bowls**
    **fork**
    **large 10-inch frying pan**
    **pancake turner**
    **plate**
    **large bowl**
    **measuring cups or glass measuring jar**
    **measuring spoons**
    **platter (for serving)**

**DIRECTIONS:**

1. Assemble ingredients and utensils.
2. Peel and chop the onion on the cutting board, then set it aside.
3. Chop the tomatoes and set them aside.
4. Using the key on the can, open and remove the corned beef. Be very careful not to cut yourself on the sharp edges

*Gari Foto*

of the can (or get an adult to help you). Crumble half of the meat into pieces with your fingers, then set it aside in a small bowl.

5.  Open the tomato sauce with the can opener and put a tablespoon of it into a small bowl. Break the 2 eggs and add them to the bowl. Use a fork to mix the eggs and tomato sauce together.

6.  Heat 2 tablespoons of peanut oil over medium heat in the frying pan. Tilt the pan a little, so the oil covers the bottom of the pan. Don't let the oil start to smoke. Add about a tablespoon of the chopped onion and fry it for just a minute, stirring constantly. Stir in the egg mixture and spread it to cover the pan. Let the mixture cook for a minute or two without touching it. Turn the heat to low, fold the egg "pancake" in half with a pancake turner, and let it cook a little longer until the egg no longer looks wet or runny. Carefully turn the egg out of the pan onto a plate. Cut it into thin strips with the knife. Turn off the stove and set the pan aside to use later.

7.  Put the 2 cups of gari into the large bowl. Measure out ¾ cup of water and add ¼ teaspoon salt to the water. Sprinkle half of the water onto the gari, mixing it in with a fork. Add more of the water until the gari is dampened, but not soaking wet. Set the bowl aside.

8.  Put the frying pan back on the stove and turn the heat to medium. Add the 2 tablespoons of palm oil, ¼ cup of peanut oil, and the rest of the chopped onion to the pan and fry the onion for a few minutes. When it becomes kind of clear, add the corned beef and cook for another minute or two. Add the chopped tomato, red pepper, and ginger. Fry all of these together for about 3 minutes, then add half of the sliced egg mixture. Carefully stir in the gari mixture and let it heat through for five minutes on low heat. While it is heating, use a fork to break up any lumps of gari. Make sure you have mixed everything well—especially the gari and stew on the bottom of the pan.

**TO SERVE:**

Spoon the gari foto onto a serving platter. Place the egg strips on top of the gari, and sprinkle chopped parsley over the top. Serve warm.

**VARIATIONS:**
1. Add 2 teaspoons of dried ground shrimp in Step 8 with the ginger and red pepper.
2. Use 4 cups of cooked rice in place of the gari, and leave out the salt and water in Step 7.
3. To reduce the preparation time, stir in all of the egg strips and omit the parsley garnish.
4. Substitute a 1-inch piece of fresh peeled ginger and a small chili pepper for the dried pepper and ginger. Grind them in a blender or food processor with about a table-spoon of water, then add them to the hot oil when frying the onion in Step 8.

# Corned Beef Stew

Using oil, red peppers, tomatoes, onions, creativity, and various other vegetables or protein sources, Ghanaians can turn out an almost endless variety of tasty stews. Stew made with canned corned beef always makes me think of Christmas. During December, many Ghanaians who work in cities or other parts of the country return to their home towns to be with their families. When they come to visit, they may bring the popular but expensive "tinned provisions" as gifts—like corned beef, sardines, or mackerel. Any of these ingredients can be turned into a delicious stew that is an African version of a hash or chowder, but without the potatoes or milk.

This recipe serves four to five people and goes well with plain boiled rice or *Rice and Beans*.

*Corned Beef Stew*

### INGREDIENTS:

- 1 tin corned beef
- ¼ teaspoon ground dried ginger
- ½ teaspoon curry powder
- ⅛ teaspoon ground red pepper
- 1 large onion
- ⅓ cup peanut oil
- 1 8-ounce can tomato sauce
- ½ teaspoon salt
- ¾ cup water
- 2 eggs
- 1 small onion (for garnish)
- 1 red or green sweet bell pepper (for garnish)
- 1 tablespoon vegetable oil (for garnish)

**UTENSILS:**

cutting board
knife
plate
measuring spoons
small bowls
fork
large frying pan with lid
pancake turner or wooden spoon
timer
can opener
small frying pan
serving bowl

**DIRECTIONS:**

1. Assemble ingredients and utensils.
2. Using the key on the bottom of the corned beef can, wind open the can, being careful not to cut yourself on the very sharp metal (or get an adult helper to do this). Turn the can upside down, slide the corned beef out onto the cutting board, and cut it into 1-inch cubes. If the corned beef does not slide out easily, use a table knife or a fork to help loosen it from the can. Put the cubes onto a plate, and set them aside.
3. Measure the ginger, curry powder, and red pepper into a small bowl and mix with a fork. Set it aside.
4. Peel and slice the onion on the cutting board.
5. Heat the ⅓ cup peanut oil in the frying pan on medium heat for 3 minutes, then add the onion and fry it for 5 minutes, stirring it with the pancake turner or wooden spoon.
6. Add the corned beef cubes and continue frying for 2 more minutes.
7. Sprinkle in the spices and stir well to coat the meat and onion. Fry for 2 more minutes.
8. Open the can of tomato sauce and stir it into the frying pan. Fry for 3 minutes, stirring a few times while it cooks.
9. Stir in the ½ teaspoon salt and ¾ cup water, then let them simmer, covered, for a few minutes while you prepare the eggs.

10. Break the eggs into the same small bowl used for the spices and beat them with a fork. Carefully uncover the stew (turn the lid away from you, so the steam does not burn you), and slowly pour in the beaten eggs, stirring constantly. By now the corned beef cubes should be falling apart. Stir for another minute, then put the lid on again and let the stew simmer for 10 minutes, stirring once after 5 minutes. The stew should be thick—not runny and watery—when it is done, so if there is still too much liquid after 10 minutes, uncover the pan and let it cook a few more minutes until most of the water has evaporated.
11. While the stew is simmering, wash the bell pepper, cut off the top, and remove the seeds; then slice it into thin rings. Peel the small onion and slice it into rings too. Heat the tablespoon of oil in the small frying pan on medium heat, and fry the onion and pepper rings for a few minutes until they are soft. Turn or stir them with a spatula while they cook. After a few minutes, turn off the heat and set them aside until you are ready to serve the stew.

## TO SERVE:

Put the stew into a serving bowl and decorate the top with the pepper and onion rings. Serve the stew spooned over individual plates of plain white rice or *Rice and Beans*.

## VARIATIONS:

1. Use canned sardines in tomato sauce or canned mackerel instead of the corned beef, and leave out the ginger and curry powder.
2. Use fresh chopped tomatoes instead of the tomato sauce. Add chopped tomatoes to the stew after the onion.
3. Leave out the sweet pepper and onion garnish.
4. Use the sweet pepper and/or onions, but do not cook them first.
5. Instead of using sweet peppers and onions, stir 1½ cups of frozen peas and carrots into the stew when you add the salt and water to the stew in Step 9.
6. Use fresh chili pepper and ginger instead of dried spices (see Variation 4 in *Gari Foto* recipe).

# Fish and Gravy

The first time he and his family visited us in Pennsylvania for a traditional North American Thanksgiving dinner, my brother-in-law kept looking around the table for the gravy. When people in Ghana talk about serving *gravy* with meat or fish, they mean something quite different from what we in the United States call gravy. We think of a brown gravy made with flour, meat or poultry drippings, and maybe milk or cream. In Ghana, the word *gravy* commonly refers to a sauce made from onions, oil, tomatoes, and pepper. Fish and Gravy is a regular dinner meal for our family. We like it with *Ampesi,* rice, or *Kenkey* and fresh fruit for dessert.

This recipe uses an electric blender or food processor to grind the vegetables for the sauce. When I first learned to grind things in Ghana, we used a specially shaped wooden spoon and a black clay bowl with ridges in it. It was especially hard for me because I am left-handed; and in Ghana, my teacher told me, you must use your right hand to grind things!

*Fish and Gravy*

**INGREDIENTS:**

1 large onion (or two medium)
1 16-ounce can tomatoes
¼ teaspoon salt
¼ teaspoon ground red pepper
¼ cup flour
1 pound frozen fish fillets, cut into 6 portions (haddock or cod)
¼ cup peanut oil
½ cup water
½ teaspoon salt

**UTENSILS:**

knife
cutting board
electric blender (or food processor)
can opener
measuring spoons
measuring cups
plate
spoon
10-inch frying pan
pancake turner
timer
serving platter
wooden spoon

**DIRECTIONS:**

1. Assemble ingredients and utensils.
2. Using the cutting board and knife, cut the ends off of the onion, peel it, and cut it into four big chunks. Put the onion chunks into the electric blender container (or bowl of the food processor).
3. Open the can of tomatoes, then add four of the tomatoes and 2 tablespoons of the juice from the can to the onion in the blender.
4. Put the lid on the blender (or food processor) and grind the tomatoes and onion on low. You might have to stop the

blender to stir or push down on the tomatoes with a wooden spoon to be sure that the tomato juice gets to the blades of the blender. Set it aside when it is blended.

5. On the plate, put ¼ teaspoon salt, ¼ teaspoon ground red pepper, and ¼ cup flour. Mix well with a spoon.

6. One by one, put the fish pieces in the flour mixture, turning them to coat them well on all sides. Stack them up on the side of the plate as you work.

7. Pour ¼ cup peanut oil into the frying pan, then heat the pan on medium to medium-high heat for about 5 minutes. (Set the timer to remind you.) Be sure that the oil does not start to smoke.

8. After the 5 minutes, carefully place the fish in a single layer in the oil in the pan. Cook for 5 minutes. (Set the timer again.) Using a pancake turner, gently turn the pieces of fish over. Be careful not to splash yourself with the hot oil. Cook the fish for another 5 minutes, or until it is cooked through.

9. Using the pancake turner, remove the fish to the serving platter.

10. Pour the tomato and onion mixture into the frying pan and cook on medium for 5 minutes, stirring with a wooden spoon or pancake turner. Turn the heat to low.

11. Grind two more tomatoes, ½ cup of the tomato juice from the can, and ½ cup water in the blender or food processor.

12. Add the ground tomatoes to the gravy in the frying pan, turn the heat back up to medium, and stir well. Add ½ teaspoon salt, and stir again. Taste the gravy with a spoon. (Don't burn your tongue!) Add more salt and ground red pepper if you like.

13. Put the fish back in the pan with the gravy for a few minutes to heat them all the way through again.

**TO SERVE:**
Carefully lift the fish portions out of the pan with the pancake turner and place them on the platter. Pour the gravy over the fish. Enjoy it with your choice of starchy accompaniment.

## VARIATIONS:

1. This can also be made using fresh peeled tomatoes instead of canned.
2. The gravy can be made without the fish and poured over any cooked meat, fish, poultry, or eggs.

# Egg Curry

This is a satisfying vegetarian main dish for lunch or a light dinner. We like it served over rice. It goes well with *Tropical Fruit Salad* for dessert. This recipe serves four to five people.

## INGREDIENTS:

5 eggs (1 per person)
1 medium onion
1 large tomato
1½ teaspoons curry powder
1 tablespoon flour
salt
1 tablespoon unsalted, dry roasted peanuts
3 tablespoons margarine
1 cup water

## UTENSILS:

small saucepan
measuring spoons
timer
slotted spoon
paring knife
cutting board
2 small bowls
frying pan
pancake turner
measuring cup
serving bowl

*Egg Curry*

**DIRECTIONS:**

1. Assemble ingredients and utensils.
2. Gently set the eggs in the saucepan, cover them with cold water, and add ¼ teaspoon salt. Slowly bring the water to a boil over medium high heat. Lower the heat to medium and cook for 10 minutes to hard boil the eggs. (Set the timer.) Remove the eggs from the water with a slotted spoon and set them aside to cool. (Older cooks can set the saucepan in the sink, pour off the hot water, and cover the eggs with cold water.)
3. Peel and chop the onion on the cutting board. Set it aside.
4. Chop the tomato, put it into a small bowl, and set it aside.
5. Measure out the curry powder and put it in a small bowl, along with the tablespoon of flour and ½ teaspoon of salt.
6. Chop the peanuts on the cutting board, then set them aside.
7. Put the 3 tablespoons of margarine into the frying pan and melt it over medium heat. When the margarine is melted,

add the chopped onion and cook it for a couple of minutes, stirring well.

8. Add the chopped tomato and stir well to mix. Cook for one minute; then add the curry and flour mixture, stirring well to blend it. Add the chopped peanuts. Slowly stir one cup of water into the sauce. Turn the heat to low, and let the curry simmer while you peel the hard-boiled eggs. Cut each egg in half, then add them to the curry sauce and let them heat up for a few minutes. Turn off the heat and pour or spoon the curry into a serving bowl.

## TO SERVE:

If you are serving the curry with rice, put a spoonful of cooked rice on each dinner plate, then add a spoonful of the curry on top of the rice. Make sure each person gets two egg halves.

## VARIATIONS:

1. Substitute a small can of tomato sauce for the chopped tomato.
2. For special occasions, chop some extra peanuts or tomato to sprinkle on top as a garnish.

## HINT:

To make your own curry powder, mix the following ingredients together in a small bowl:

**1 teaspoon ground coriander**
**¼ teaspoon ground allspice**
**¼ teaspoon garlic powder**
**1 teaspoon ground cumin**
**½ teaspoon ground ginger**
**1 teaspoon tumeric**
**⅛ teaspoon chili powder**

If you want a spicy curry powder, add ⅛ teaspoon red pepper. Be sure to use only 1½ teaspoons of the curry powder for this recipe. Save the rest for another time.

# Bean Stew

Black-eyed peas are a type of cowpea. They are an important source of protein in Ghana, where they are often cooked in a stew with a little smoked fish. Bean Stew is a favorite dinner in our house, where we serve it with *Gari* or fried ripe plantain. However, it could just as well be served with plain boiled rice. It keeps and reheats well, so it can be made ahead of time. This meal is quite filling, and a light fruit dessert is all that is needed to complete it.

**INGREDIENTS:**

    **1 cup dried black-eyed peas**
    **water**
    **½ teaspoon salt**
    **1 medium onion**
    **1 8-ounce can tomato sauce**
    **½ pound smoked fish (smoked whiting, haddock, or whitefish)**
    **⅓ cup red palm oil**
    **⅛ teaspoon ground red pepper**

**UTENSILS:**

    **colander**
    **bowl**
    **2-quart saucepan**
    **measuring cups**
    **timer**
    **measuring spoons**
    **paring knife**
    **cutting board**
    **can opener**
    **frying pan**
    **pancake turner**
    **serving bowl and spoon**

*Bean Stew*

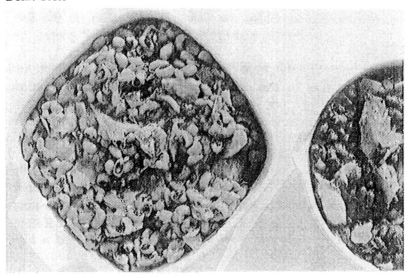

## DIRECTIONS:

1. Assemble ingredients and utensils.
2. The night before you want to eat the stew, put the beans in a colander and pick through them, throwing away any that are spoiled or look "yucky." Pick out any small stones that might be mixed in with them. Rinse the beans well with cold water.
3. Put the beans into a bowl and cover them with 3 cups of water. Leave the beans to soak overnight in the refrigerator.
4. The next day, put the beans and water into a pot. Use a spoon to scoop off and discard any floating bean "skins." Add another cup of water to the pot. Bring the water to a boil over high heat; then lower the heat to simmer, cover the pan, and let the beans cook slowly until they are tender—it will take about an hour. Be sure to check them every half hour to make sure that the beans don't cook dry. Add more water if necessary. The beans are done when they are soft and tender.
5. After the beans are cooked, add the salt to the water.

6. Peel the onion, then slice or chop it. Open the can of tomato sauce. Rinse the fish. Peel the skin off the fish, remove the bones, and break the fish into small pieces. Set aside.

7. In the frying pan, heat the ⅓ cup oil over medium heat. Add the onions to the oil, and fry them until they become "see-through," or translucent. It will just take a few minutes. Stir them with the pancake turner, so they don't burn; then slowly pour the tomato sauce into the pan and stir well. Add the fish next, and stir it together. Let it cook for a few minutes, then spoon the sauce into the pan with the beans. Add the ⅛ teaspoon red pepper and ½ to 1 cup of water. Simmer the stew for about 20 minutes on low heat. Stir it a few times while it is cooking. Taste it to see if there is enough salt and red pepper for you, and add a little more if you want.

**TO SERVE:**

Spoon the stew into a serving bowl, and eat it on a plate with *Gari*, fried ripe plantain, or boiled rice.

**VARIATIONS:**

1. Use two 15-ounce cans of black-eyed peas (drained) instead of 1 cup of dried beans.
2. Substitute red aduki beans for the black-eyed peas. These beans take longer to cook, so allow extra time.
3. Use 1½ tablespoons dried minced onions for the fresh onions, but do not fry the dried onions—add them to the beans after you have made the tomato and oil sauce.
4. Use smoked ham cubes or ham hocks instead of smoked fish. If you use ham hocks, you may cook them along with the beans.
5. Use peanut oil, corn oil, or some other vegetable oil instead of palm oil.
6. Use 1 cup of pureed tomatoes or a small can of tomato paste plus ½ cup of water in the place of the tomato sauce.

**HINT:**

A faster way to get the beans ready is to put them in a pan with the water after washing them, bring the water to a boil over high heat, boil for 2 minutes, then take the pan off the burner (turn off the stove!), cover it, and let the beans soak for one hour. After the hour, continue with Step 4.

# Meat Stew

People in Africa do not always use special measuring cups to measure ingredients. Instead, they often use whatever containers they have handy. For example, someone from Ghana might say to add "one small tomato sauce can of water" to this stew. Because a tomato sauce can holds eight ounces, it is the same as one cup.

This is a good everyday kind of stew that goes equally well with rice, *Ampesi,* or mashed potatoes.

*Meat Stew*

**INGREDIENTS:**

- 2 tablespoons flour
- 1 pound meat (chuck roast, stewing beef, or flank steak)
- 1 medium onion
- 1 8-ounce can tomato sauce
- 2 tablespoons cooking oil (peanut or corn oil)
- 1 teaspoon salt
- ⅛ teaspoon ground red pepper
- 1 cup water
- 1 teaspoon beef bouillon granules

**UTENSILS:**

- 10-inch frying pan and lid
- measuring spoons
- timer
- small bowl
- cutting board
- knife
- can opener
- pancake turner (spatula)
- measuring cup

**DIRECTIONS:**

1. Assemble ingredients and utensils.
2. Put a clean, empty frying pan on the stove and turn the heat to medium. After 3 minutes, sprinkle the 2 tablespoons of flour into the pan. Stir or gently shake the pan until the white flour turns brown. It will probably take about 5 to 10 minutes. Be careful not to burn the flour. Pour the flour into a small bowl and set it aside. Turn off the heat and remove the pan from the hot burner.
3. Slice the meat into thin slices on the cutting board and set it aside.
4. Peel and chop the onion on the cutting board.
5. Open the can of tomato sauce.
6. Pour 2 tablespoons of oil into the frying pan, then heat the oil over medium heat for 2 or 3 minutes. Stir in the meat

and brown it over medium or medium-high heat. Turn the meat so both sides brown, and stir it a few times as it cooks. This will take about 5 to 10 minutes. Add a little more oil if it starts to stick.

7. Add the chopped onion to the meat, and continue cooking and stirring for about 5 minutes more.
8. Stir in the tomato sauce.
9. Add the salt, red pepper, water, and teaspoon of beef bouillon, then stir well. (You can use one tomato sauce can to measure the water.)
10. Sprinkle the browned flour over the stew and stir well. Lower the heat to simmer, cover the frying pan with the lid, and cook for 30 minutes or until the meat is tender. Stir the stew after 15 minutes, and add a little more water if necessary.
11. Just before serving, check to see if the stew has enough salt and pepper for you. If not, add ¼ to ½ teaspoon salt and a dash of red pepper.

**TO SERVE:**

Fill a serving bowl with the stew, then ladle it over plain boiled rice or mashed potatoes, or serve it alongside ampesi. It is nice to serve it with red pepper flakes on the table for people to add if they want it spicier.

**VARIATIONS:**

1. Meat Stew is also good if you add a few cups of fresh sliced mushrooms when you brown the meat and onions. Add 2 tablespoons more oil.
2. Try adding a package of frozen chopped spinach while the meat is simmering.
3. Younger cooks might want to skip browning the flour (Step 1) and just sprinkle it in unbrowned in Step 9.
4. For a stew that is not so spicy, leave out the red pepper or use just a dash instead of ⅛ teaspoon.

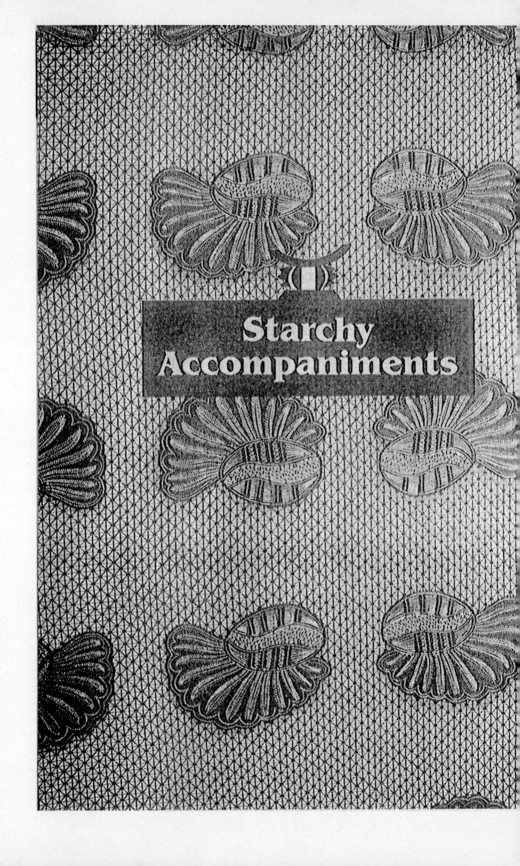

# Starchy Accompaniments

# Rice Balls

Rice balls are a fun way to serve rice with a bowl of soup or stew. They are also easy to make.

**INGREDIENTS:**

> **1 cup long-grain white rice (not precooked)**
> **3 ½ cups water**
> **1 teaspoon salt**

**UTENSILS:**

> **3-quart saucepan or pot with lid**
> **measuring spoon**
> **measuring cup**
> **fork**
> **long-handled wooden spoon**
> **potato masher (ricer)**
> **ice cream scoop**
> **cup**
> **timer**
> **serving bowl or platter**

**DIRECTIONS:**

1. Assemble the ingredients and utensils.
2. Put the rice, water, and salt into a large pot, stir it once or twice with a fork, then set the pot on the stove. Turn the burner to high, and bring the water and rice to a boil.
3. When it starts to boil, reduce the heat to low and cover the pot. Allow the rice to cook for about 20 minutes. (Set the timer.) After 20 minutes, remove the cover carefully, so the steam doesn't burn you, and taste the rice to see if it is cooked. Stir the rice with the wooden spoon to make sure that it has not stuck to the bottom of the pot and scorched or burned. If the rice does not taste cooked, cover it again and let it cook for a few more minutes. If it seems dry, add a little more water.

4. When the rice is cooked, turn off the stove and let the rice sit uncovered for a few minutes to cool slightly. Then, using a potato masher or a strong wooden spoon, stir and mash the rice until it is fairly smooth. Fill a cup with cold water. Dip an ice cream scoop in the water, then scoop up a ball of the mashed rice and place it on a serving platter. Dip the scoop back in the water and repeat the process until the rice is all made into balls (one cup of rice makes about nine balls). If you do not have an ice cream scoop, place spoonfuls of rice on a plate to cool. When they are cool enough to hold, wet your hands slightly with water and form the spoonfuls of rice into balls with your hands. They will look like snow balls. If the balls fall apart, you need to cook the rice a little longer until more of the water is absorbed.

5. As you make them, put the rice balls on a serving platter or pile them gently into a serving bowl.

**TO SERVE:**

Place a rice ball in an individual bowl of soup or stew—like *Peanut Butter Soup, Palaver Sauce,* or *Light Soup.*

*Rice Balls*

**VARIATIONS:**

To simply cook plain boiled rice, put 1 cup of rice into the pot with the teaspoon of salt and only 2 cups of water. Cover the pan and bring the water and rice to a boil, then lower the heat to medium or low and simmer for about 20 minutes, until the rice is cooked. Do not shape the rice into balls.

# Gari

Read about this handy African "fast food" in the ingredients glossary at the beginning of this book. Gari is one thing you will have to prepare with imported ingredients. It is delicious with *Bean Stew*. But beware—it is very filling and a little goes a long way.

**INGREDIENTS:**
   1¼ cups gari
   2 cups water

**UTENSILS:**
   measuring cups
   coarse strainer or flour sifter
   bowl (large enough to hold the gari)
   fork
   saucepan or microwave-safe pitcher
   pitcher or teapot

**DIRECTIONS:**
1. Assemble the ingredients and utensils.
2. The texture of the gari in Ghana is quite fine, but the gari that is imported to the U.S. is often coarser, so we use a strainer or sieve to sift the gari into a bowl. Just shake the strainer and hit it with one hand or stir the gari inside the strainer with a spoon to help it fall through the strainer. It may take about 1¼ cups of gari from a package to end up with 1 cup after sifting it.

3.  Heat 2 cups of water to boiling in a saucepan on the stove or in a pitcher in the microwave oven. Pour the boiling water into a serving pitcher or teapot. Spoon a few tablespoons of gari onto a plate. Pour the hot water onto the gari. We like our gari soft, so we usually add at least as much water as gari—perhaps even twice as much. The gari will absorb the water and swell up.

**TO SERVE:**

At the table, use a fork to mix up the water and gari, then add a few spoonfuls of stew to the side of the gari. Our children often prefer to mix the gari and stew together; but the traditional way to eat it is to take a bite of stew and gari together, and let the mixing take place inside your mouth.

# Fufu

In North America, we might serve thick slices of bread or biscuits with a steaming bowl of hearty soup or beef stew. In Ghana and much of West Africa, soup is often ladled over boiled and pounded yams, plantains, cassava, or a combination of two, like cassava and plantain. The starchy vegetables are peeled and boiled like *Ampesi*, but then they are pounded and turned and pounded and turned and pounded and turned in a wooden mortar with a long wooden pestle. When they are ready, they are formed into balls—like a cross between a heavy dumpling and a thick porridge. Whenever I think of Ghana, I remember the soothing sound of people chatting and pounding fufu for the evening meal.

People from Ghana who travel abroad—leaving their wooden mortars and pestles behind—make do with an "American-style" fufu by substituting instant mashed potatoes and potato starch flour for the yams. In stores that carry African foods, you can

*Fufu*

find expensive imported instant fufu made from yam, plantain, and cassava, to which you simply add hot water.

Fufu is never eaten alone—soup or a thick stew is always poured over it. To eat the fufu, you take a small piece of fufu dipped in the soup, and swallow it without chewing. Soup and fufu is one of my all-time favorite meals, but it is one I learned to like by first trying it several times.

This recipe makes enough fufu for four to six people to try.

**INGREDIENTS:**
> **1 cup potato starch flour**
> **2 cups instant mashed potato**
> **4 to 5 cups water**

**UTENSILS:**
> **measuring cups**
> **3-quart saucepan**
> **sturdy wooden spoon or spatula**
> **cup**
> **small bowl**
> **serving platter**

**DIRECTIONS:**
1. Assemble ingredients and utensils.
2. Measure the cup of potato starch flour into the saucepan.
3. Add 2 cups of instant mashed potatoes to the potato starch and mix well with the wooden spoon.
4. Add 4 cups of cold water to the potato mixture and stir well.
5. Fill a cup with water and set it near the stove where you will cook the fufu.
6. Put the saucepan on the stove, turn the heat to medium, and stir constantly in a "figure eight" motion while it cooks: Hold the handle of the pan while you stir the fufu. It will probably take about 15 to 20 minutes for the fufu to become stiff and springy. This fufu is a lot easier to make than pounded fufu, but it still takes a strong arm to turn

and scrape the bottom of the pan for so long. Also, the stirrer has to be careful not to get too enthusiastic at the beginning, or the fufu will spill over the edge of the pan. The extra water is near the stove in case the fufu gets too dry and starts to stick to the bottom of the pan. If this happens, add a couple of tablespoons of water at a time while you stir.

**TO SERVE:**

Let the fufu pan cool for a few minutes, so you won't burn your fingers. There are two ways to make the fufu balls.

1. Scoop spoonfuls of the fufu into individual soup bowls, and spoon soup directly over the top of the fufu.
2. Mold balls of fufu and put them on a moistened serving platter. To mold the balls, you need a cup of water and a small bowl. Sprinkle a little water in the bowl to keep the fufu from sticking to it; then dip the bowl into the pan of fufu and scoop up a bowlful. Wet your hands with water, shape the fufu in the bowl into a flat oval ball, and put it on the serving platter. Repeat until all the fufu is shaped.

Serve the fufu balls with *Light Soup, Peanut Butter Soup,* or *Palmnut Soup.* Always pour the soup over the top of the fufu balls, so they are covered with a glaze of soup in your bowl.

# Ampesi
# (Boiled Starchy Vegetables)

Lunch or dinner in Ghana is often a stew served with boiled starchy vegetables such as yams, plantains, or cassava. These boiled vegetables are known in the Twi language as *ampesi.* In the United States, we generally substitute potatoes for the

African yams, and eat ampesi made from potatoes and plantains. The plantains can be green, half-ripe, or completely ripe. The ripe ones are sweeter, softer, and much easier to peel, and our children prefer them to the green ones.

In ampesi, usually all the different kinds of vegetables are boiled together in the same pot. My sister-in-law, Afua, taught me to put the vegetables that take longest to cook, like cocoyams, on the bottom of the pot and the softer vegetables above them. Once, when we were in Ghana staying at a guest house, an important visitor known as *Nana*, which means "king" or "chief," stayed at the same place. Each of his vegetables had to be boiled in a separate kettle placed over the charcoal fire.

For each person, plan on one large potato and half of a large plantain. This recipe serves four people.

**INGREDIENTS:**
- **4 large potatoes**
- **2 large plantains (green or ripe)**
  - **water**
- **1 teaspoon salt**

**UTENSILS:**
- **vegetable peeler**
- **paring knife**
- **cutting board**
- **large kettle with lid**
- **measuring spoon**
- **timer**
- **fork**
- **long-handled slotted spoon**
- **serving plate**

**DIRECTIONS:**
1. Assemble the ingredients and utensils.
2. Rinse the potatoes, peel them with the vegetable peeler, then cut them in half and in half again. Put them into the kettle.

3. Peel the plantains (see recipe for *Plantain Chips* for directions on how to peel a plantain). Cut them into 2-inch chunks, and add them to the kettle.
4. Put enough water in the kettle to cover the vegetables, then put the kettle on the stove. It will be heavy, so you may need an adult helper.
5. Turn the heat to high, add a teaspoon of salt to the water, and cover the kettle with a lid. Bring the water to a boil over high heat.
6. When the water boils, turn the heat down to medium-high and cook for 20 minutes (set the timer), or until the vegetables feel soft when poked with a fork. To check the vegetables, be careful to tilt the lid of the kettle away from you when you uncover the pot, so the steam doesn't burn you.
7. When the vegetables are cooked, you can turn off the heat and lift them out of the water with a slotted spoon. (Older cooks, or those with adult helpers, may want to drain the extra water off by pouring it down the sink, instead of lifting the vegetables out of the water individually.)

*Ampesi (Boiled Starchy Vegetables)*

**TO SERVE:**

Arrange the vegetables on a platter and serve with a stew, such as *Palaver Sauce* or *Meat Stew.*

**VARIATIONS:**

Use American yams or sweet potatoes instead of (or along with) the plantains. Cook them the same way you cook the potatoes (shown in photograph).

# Kenkey

Kenkey and Banku are both staple dishes made from a cornmeal dough.

When I first lived in Africa, I stayed in a small town along the coast of Ghana, not far from the capital city of Accra. Many people from the ethnic group known as Ga live there, and that is where I grew to love kenkey and fried fish. To make kenkey, cornmeal is "soured" like wheat flour to make sourdough starter in the United States. The fermented cornmeal dough is formed into balls that are wrapped in corn husks or plantain or banana leaves and steamed. There are different names and different versions of kenkey (or *kenke*)—it is called *komi* among the Ga-speaking people, and *dokono* by the Twi-speaking Akan people. Kenkey has a special sour taste and is commonly served with fried fish and a hot pepper sauce called *shito*. It is also eaten with many soups or stews. Try it with *Palaver Sauce, Groundnut Stew, Meat Stew,* or *Fish and Gravy.*

In Ghana, kenkey is eaten with your hands—like we might eat a hamburger or French fries. However, learning how to eat any starch and soup or stew this way without spilling (and without neglecting details like how to wash your hands first and afterward) is a skill that must be learned—just like learning to eat with chopsticks. For North Americans, it is acceptable to take a spoonful of stew and kenkey together and eat it like we might eat soup and dumplings, or, even better, you might find an African and ask her or him to teach you how!

You need three things to succeed in making kenkey. First, you need patience and the ability to wait a day or two for the corn dough to ferment. Second, you must have the right ingredients. When I first tried to make kenkey and banku in the United States, I failed many times because I used the wrong kind of cornmeal. Do not use regular degerminated cornmeal, and don't try masa harina. Instead, look for the finely ground white cornmeal used in the South—like stone-ground white cornmeal. Third, you need a strong arm to keep turning the dough while it is cooking. With these three things in mind (or in hand), you should have no problem.

**INGREDIENTS:**
   **3 cups fine white stone-ground cornmeal**
   **1 tablespoon cornstarch**
   **3 cups warm water**
   **2 cups boiling water**
   **1 teaspoon salt**

**UTENSILS:**
   **measuring cup**
   **measuring spoons**
   **large ceramic or glass bowl (not metal)**
   **wooden spoon or paddle**
   **waxed paper or cloth**
   **3-quart saucepan**
   **aluminum foil**
   **large pan with steamer insert and cover**
   **timer**
   **potholder**

**DIRECTIONS:**
1. Assemble ingredients and utensils.
2. Measure 3 cups of cornmeal and 1 tablespoon cornstarch into the bowl.

3. Add 3 cups of warm water and mix well with your hand or a wooden spoon. We prefer to use our right hand like they would in Ghana. Pat the dough smooth.
4. Cover the bowl loosely with a piece of cloth or waxed paper to protect it from dust, and set it aside in a warm place (next to the stove or inside the oven if you are not using it) for a day or two to allow it to ferment. The longer you leave the dough, the sharper the sour taste becomes.
5. A day or two after making the dough, (when you are ready to make the kenkey) use a spoon to carefully scrape off any mold that might have grown on top of the dough. Throw the moldy part away. Divide the corn dough in half.
6. Measure 2 cups of water into a 3-quart saucepan, then bring it to a boil over high heat. When it boils, add the teaspoon of salt and turn the heat down to medium.
7. Add one half of the corn dough to the water, then mix and cook it for 10 minutes, stirring carefully to keep it from scorching or burning.
8. Remove the pan from the heat and stir in the uncooked portion of corn dough. Mix them together well.
9. Tear off three or four large squares of aluminum foil, about 10 inches square. Divide the dough into 3 or 4 large spoonfuls, and put one spoonful on each of the aluminum squares.
10. Wet your hands, and use them to shape the dough into balls. Pull the corners of the foil up around the dough ball and twist them together at the top, leaving a little room for the ball of kenkey to expand as it steams. Repeat for each of the squares of foil.
11. Put hot water in the steamer pot and set the steamer rack in place. Put the foil packages in the rack in a single layer and cover the steamer pot.
12. Bring the water in the steamer kettle to a boil over high heat, then reduce the heat to low and steam the kenkey for about an hour and a half. Check every half hour or so during the cooking time to make sure there is still water in the steamer.

**TO SERVE:**

After the kenkey is steamed, it may be served either hot or cold. Allow the packages to cool slightly before opening and serving them, so the kenkey is firm. After the kenkey balls cool, they may be sliced into several servings and eaten with soup or stew.

**VARIATIONS:**
1. Sometimes, instead of balls, the kenkey is rolled and shaped into logs.
2. In some places, balls of unfermented corn dough are also steamed. After making the dough, follow the directions for kenkey without waiting for the dough to sour. It may be necessary to decrease the boiling water by ¼ cup.
3. You can leave out the cornstarch, but the dough will not be quite as smooth.
4. People who are used to the fermented taste might want to wait three to five days before cooking the corn dough. If you keep the corn dough this long, check it every morning for mold. If there is none, stir the dough well with a wooden spoon once each day. If there is any mold growing, scrape it off completely and throw it away before stirring the dough.
5. At the school where I taught, the girls would sometimes crumble kenkey into a cup and mix it with evaporated milk, sugar cubes, and cold water to make a filling drink for a snack.

# Banku

Banku is made from the same fermented corn dough as *Kenkey*, but the dough is cooked differently, so banku is softer. Banku is also usually eaten with a stew or soup. Try it with *Palmnut Soup, Peanut Butter Stew, Meat Stew, Vegetarian Ground-nut Soup,* or *Palaver Sauce.* This recipe makes enough for four

*Kenkey (left) and Banku (right)*

or five North American-sized servings, but two Africans could probably finish it off easily.

**INGREDIENTS:**
>2 cups fine white stoneground cornmeal
>2 teaspoons cornstarch
>water
>1 teaspoon salt

**UTENSILS:**
>1¾-quart ceramic or glass bowl (not metal)
>measuring cup
>measuring spoon
>sturdy wooden spoon or paddle
>waxed paper or cloth
>3-quart saucepan

## DIRECTIONS:

1. Assemble ingredients and utensils.
2. Measure 2 cups of cornmeal and 2 teaspoons of cornstarch into the bowl.
3. Add 2 cups of warm (not hot) water from the faucet to the bowl, and mix well with your hand or a wooden spoon. Pat the dough smooth.
4. Cover the bowl loosely with waxed paper or a cloth to protect it, set it aside in a warm place away from drafts, and leave it for one or two nights.
5. The day you are ready to cook the banku (one or two days later), first make sure no mold has grown on top of the dough. If any has, scrape it off with a spoon and throw that part away.
6. Put a cup of water into a 3-quart saucepan and bring it to a boil over high heat. When the water boils, lower the heat to medium.
7. Add the teaspoon of salt and the corn dough to the water.
8. Mix the dough into the boiling water and stir it well while it cooks. It takes a strong arm and *persistence* (that means don't give up!) to keep stirring and turning the dough for 15 or 20 minutes, until the dough is cooked and stiff. It also takes a strong, flat wooden spoon or paddle—a flimsy one will break. It is important to prevent the banku from burning or scorching in the pan, so keep scraping the bottom of the pan with the spoon or paddle as the banku cooks. You can turn down the heat or add ¼ cup more water if necessary.
9. Once the banku is cooked, you can turn off the heat and let it sit for a few minutes. When it is cool enough to handle, wet your hands to keep it from sticking to them, and shape the banku into one large or several small ovals. Banku is usually eaten warm or lukewarm.

## TO SERVE:

Put the soup or stew in a serving bowl and put the banku on a serving platter. Each person may put the banku right in the bowl with the soup or alongside the stew on the plate. Just dip a small spoonful of it into your soup or stew and eat them together. In Ghana, banku is most commonly eaten with okro stew, a thick, slippery stew.

**VARIATIONS:**

Skip the souring process, and make the banku immediately after mixing the dough.

# Rice and Beans

Rice and Beans is a nice high-protein change of pace from regular rice, and the "beans" used are not really beans, but cowpeas. (See the ingredients glossary at the beginning of the book.) It goes well with any of the stews—especially *Corned Beef Stew.*

The first time I ate Rice and Beans was shortly after I arrived in Ghana in 1971 to teach at a boarding school. The children were excited that I wanted to come to the cafeteria and eat lunch with them—but they warned me that, along with stew, we were having "rice and stones." The rice and beans were thoroughly cooked, so I decided that they meant that the cooks had not carefully washed and picked through the large quantities of rice, and had left a few small stones for unlucky diners. School cafeteria lunches are the same everywhere!

**INGREDIENTS:**

- 1 10-ounce package frozen black-eyed peas
- 6 cups water
- 2 cups long-grain white rice
- 2 teaspoons salt
- ¼ cup corn oil margarine (that is 4 tablespoons or ½ a stick)

**UTENSILS:**

**5-quart pot with lid**
**measuring cup**
**teaspoon**
**bowl**
**fork**
**timer**

## DIRECTIONS:

1.  Assemble ingredients and utensils.
2.  Open the package of frozen blackeyed peas and pour them into a large 5-quart pot along with 1 cup of water. Cover the pot and bring it to a boil on high heat.
3.  While the pot heats, measure out 2 cups of long-grain white rice into a bowl. Do not use precooked rice, and do not wash the rice unless the package directions say to wash it.
4.  Carefully lift the lid on the pot, so the steam does not burn you, and add the rice to the pot along with 5 cups of water, 2 teaspoons of salt, and ¼ cup corn oil margarine. Stir a few times with a fork.

*Rice and Beans*

5. Cover the pot again and return the water to a boil. It will only take a few minutes.
6. Reduce the heat to low and cook without lifting the lid for 20 minutes (set a timer).
7. Stir the rice and beans with a fork, then continue cooking for another 5 or 10 minutes, until the beans are soft and all the water is absorbed.

**TO SERVE:**

Put the rice and beans onto a serving platter or into a serving bowl. Spoon them onto a plate and top with a spoonful of stew, or place the stew to the side of the rice and beans.

**VARIATIONS:**

1. Use no margarine or use vegetable oil instead of margarine.
2. Use 2 cups of coconut milk and 4 cups of water instead of the oil and 6 cups of water. To make coconut milk, open and prepare a fresh coconut as explained in the *Fresh Coconut* recipe. Save the liquid from the coconut. Grate the white coconut meat and put it into a bowl. Pour 1 cup of boiling water over the grated coconut and let it stand for half an hour. Line a colander with cheesecloth and put the colander over a bowl. Pour the water and coconut into the colander to strain the liquid from the meat. Pick up the ends of the cheesecloth and twist it to get more liquid out of the coconut meat. Pour this liquid (it is coconut milk) into the reserved liquid from the coconut. Shake the grated coconut meat back into a bowl, pour another cup of boiling water over it, and repeat the waiting and straining process. You can sometimes find unsweetened canned coconut milk in the store.
3. Use canned or cooked dried beans instead of frozen black-eyed peas.
4. Add any or all of the following: 1 tablespoon finely chopped onion (or a little onion powder or dried minced onion), 1 teaspoon crushed or chopped garlic (or ¼ teaspoon garlic powder), and ½ teaspoon dried thyme.

5. For special occasions, lightly rub margarine or vegetable oil in a ring mold or bowl, then firmly pack the rice and beans into it to shape it. Turn it onto a plain platter or one covered with lettuce (see the photograph).

# Fried Red Plantain Slices

In Ghana, ripe plantain is also known as red plantain. Although the outside peeling is yellow or yellow and black, the ripe plantain inside has a reddish tint to it. Ripe plantains are delicious cooked many different ways. Some recipes in this book include *Ampesi,* in which they are boiled, or *Kelewele,* in which they are cut into small cubes, mixed with spices, and deep fried. Here is another way our family (and many people in West Africa) enjoy eating them.

When they are cut into thick slices and fried, red plantains make a tasty accompaniment to stews and are very popular with children in West Africa. Fried ripe plantain goes especially well with *Bean Stew.* Plan on serving about one soft fully ripe plantain for each person. If they are very large, however, two plantains may serve three people.

**INGREDIENTS:**
   plantain(s)
   water
   salt
   cooking oil (peanut, palm, or any vegetable oil)

**UTENSILS:**
   bowl
   frying pan
   pancake turner
   paper towels or brown paper
   ½ teaspoon
   slotted spoon
   absorbent dish towel or paper towels
   serving platter

**DIRECTIONS:**

1. Assemble ingredients and utensils.
2. Cut the ends off the plantains and peel them.
3. Cut each plantain into several thick diagonal slices.

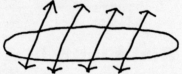

4. Soak the plantain slices in a bowl of water with about ½ teaspoon salt in it for a few minutes.
5. While the plantains soak, heat ¼ inch of oil in the frying pan over medium-high heat. Make sure the oil does not begin to smoke.
6. After about 5 minutes, use a slotted spoon to remove the plantain slices onto a dishtowel or paper towels to blot up the extra water.
7. Place a single layer of plantain slices in the hot oil in the

*Fried Red Plantain Slices (left) and Roasted Ripe Plantain (right)*

pan. If you are cooking several plantains, you may need to do it in two or three batches. Lower the heat to medium, cook the plantains until the bottoms are nicely browned, then carefully turn the slices and fry until the other sides are also brown.

8.  Remove the plantain slices with the turner or slotted spoon. Drain the fried plantain on paper towels or brown paper.

**TO SERVE:**

Put the drained slices onto a serving plate. Serve while still warm with bean or other stew. If you are frying many plantains, keep the serving platter warm by keeping it in the oven set at warm or 200 degrees.

# Roasted Ripe Plantain

This is one easy way to use up plantains that have gotten overly ripe, but not rotten, and soft and mostly black on the outside, but not moldy or spoiled on the inside. If you are planning on having the plantain as a snack, one large plantain may be enough for two people. The plantain should be soft and yellow or yellow and black.

**INGREDIENTS:**
    plantain(s)

**UTENSILS:**
    knife
    cutting board
    cookie sheet
    timer
    potholders
    serving plate

## DIRECTIONS:

1. Assemble ingredients and utensils.
2. Put the oven rack on the lowest position in the oven.
3. Preheat the oven to 425 degrees.
4. Slice off the ends of each plantain, but do not peel it.
5. Cut each plantain into four to six equal pieces, then set them on a cookie sheet with the peel touching the pan.
6. Put the cookie sheet in the oven and bake for 20 minutes. The peel will start to look like charcoal, and will become very black, but the plantain inside should not burn.
7. After 20 minutes, use a potholder to remove the hot cookie sheet (don't forget to turn off the oven) and set it on a heatproof surface. Use a spoon or your hands to put the plantain pieces onto a serving plate. Be careful because the plantain is *very hot.*

## TO SERVE:

Each person takes a few pieces of plantain and carefully removes the peel. The roasted plantain tastes good by itself or with peanuts or a stew. Our unconventional son D.K. likes to dip it in ketchup.

## VARIATIONS:

1. Partly ripe or green plantains can be cooked the same way. Because they are not as sweet, however, you might prefer to eat them with a sauce or stew.
2. Peeled sliced plantains can be roasted the same way, but you must grease the cookie sheet lightly before putting the plantain on it. You also need to use a fork to turn the plantain pieces after 10 minutes.

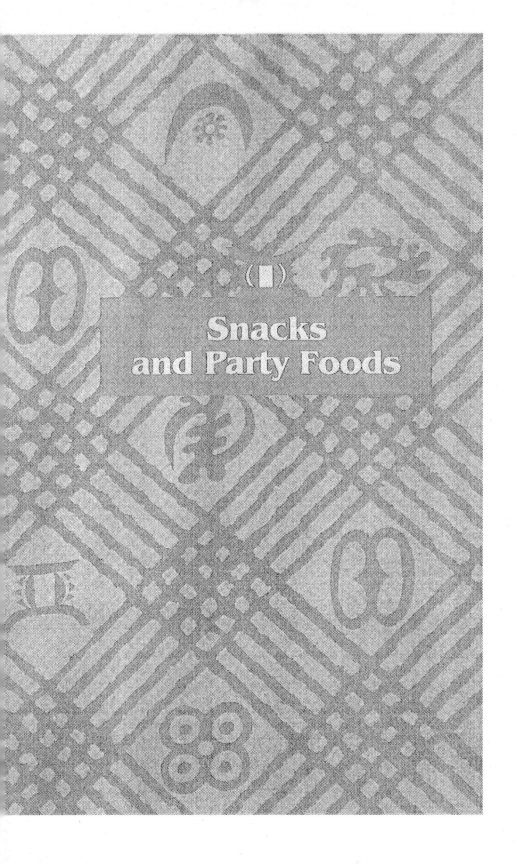

# Snacks
# and Party Foods

# Boiled Corn

Corn is eaten throughout Africa. It is a food that travelled from the Americas to Africa many, many years ago. Two common African ways of preparing foods, including corn, are boiling and roasting. When it is in season in Ghana, women often sit by the roadside with large pots or barbecue grills and sell boiled or roasted ears of corn as a snack food. In Ghana, corn is not served with butter or margarine. Instead, for a treat, people like to eat it along with chunks of fresh coconut.

Every year, our family plants a few rows of Pennsylvania's own "silver queen" corn in our garden. We look forward eating sweet white corn freshly cooked, just like people do in Ghana.

**INGREDIENTS:**

> **1 ear of sweet corn for each person (white corn if available)**
> **water**
> **salt**

**UTENSILS:**

> **large kettle**
> **teaspoon**
> **tongs or slotted spoon**
> **timer**
> **serving plate**

**DIRECTIONS:**

1. Assemble ingredients and utensils.
2. Pull off any green leaves on the corn. The leaves are called "husks" or "shucks," and taking them off is called "husking" or "shucking" the corn.
3. Rub or pull off the silky threads under the leaves, then rinse the corn under cold water and set it aside.
4. Fill a large pot half full of water. We use about 2 cups of water for each ear of corn. Add salt to the water. We use 1 teaspoon for every three ears of corn.

5. Put the pot on the stove and turn the heat to high. Wait until the water is almost boiling. It will take about 10 minutes.
6. Using tongs or the slotted spoon, carefully slide the corn into the water, then let it boil for 5 to 7 minutes. Do not splatter yourself with hot water! Set a timer to make sure you don't cook the corn too long.
7. After about 7 minutes, turn off the heat and remove the corn to a serving plate using the tongs or slotted spoon.

**TO SERVE:**

As soon as the corn is cool enough to hold in your hands, enjoy it.

**VARIATIONS:**

For a new experience, serve the corn with pieces of coconut (see the recipe for Fresh Coconut).

*Boiled and Roasted Corn*

# Roasted Corn

One of the differences between much of the corn that is eaten in Africa and the sweet corn in the United States, is that the American corn tends to be much softer and cooks more quickly. Corn that is cooked in the microwave has a chewier texture that makes it taste more like African corn. It is also quick and easy to prepare this snack.

**INGREDIENTS:**

**1 ear of sweet corn for each person (white corn if available)**

**UTENSILS:**

**microwave-safe plate**

**DIRECTIONS:**
1. Follow Step 1 and Step 2 under the directions for *Boiled Corn* to get the corn ready.
2. Put the clean corn on a microwave-safe plate in the microwave oven. Cook two ears together for 13 to 15 minutes or one ear for 5 to 7 minutes. The exact time depends on the size of the corn and how fast your microwave cooks.

**TO SERVE:**

Serve it straight from the plate as soon as it is cool enough to handle.

**VARIATIONS:**
1. If you prefer your corn softer, wrap each ear in waxed paper before cooking it.
2. Try the corn with a handful of dry roasted peanuts on the side.
3. Roast the husked corn a few inches above hot coals on a barbecue grill, turning it as it cooks, until it is browned on each side.

# Chichinga
# (Grilled Pieces of Meat)

This popular African snack and party food is similar to, but spicier than the shish kebabs we have in North America. The crushed peanuts give it a fresh twist.

Chichinga apparently is known by many other names, depending on where you are in West Africa. It is *chachanga* in Togo, *suya* or *tsire agashi* in Nigeria, or also *kyinkyinga* in Ghana. When we were in Ghana in 1984, we always loved to go anywhere that Chichinga was being barbecued. By the way, it is delicious to eat while sipping ginger beer or any of the squashes (lemon, lime, or orange).

## INGREDIENTS:
1 pound roundsteak (or other tender cut of beef)
½ cup dry roasted unsalted peanuts
¼ teaspoon ground dried red pepper (or ⅛ teaspoon dried red pepper and ⅛ teaspoon paprika)
½ teaspoon ground dried ginger
½ teaspoon salt
¼ cup peanut or other vegetable oil

## UTENSILS:
knife
cutting board
plate
waxed paper
measuring cup
rolling pin (or meat tenderizer)
small bowl
measuring spoons
spoon
pastry brush
platter
broiling pan
timer

**oven gloves or potholders**
**fork**
**serving spoon**
**toothpicks (optional)**

## DIRECTIONS:

1.  Assemble ingredients and utensils.
2.  Cut the meat into ½-inch cubes using the knife and cutting board. Pile the cubes onto the plate and set it aside.
3.  Preheat the broiler, making sure the broiler pan will be about 3 or 4 inches from the broiler coils.
4.  Tear off a piece of waxed paper about 2 feet long, set it on a table or countertop, and pour the peanuts onto the paper. Cover the peanuts with another piece of waxed paper. Crush the peanuts finely by rolling the rolling pin over them until they are small powdery pieces. (If you have a meat tenderizer, gently pound the peanuts with the smooth side of the meat tenderizer.) Pour the crushed peanuts into a small bowl.
5.  Add the red pepper (or red pepper and paprika), ginger, and salt to the crushed peanuts in the small bowl, then stir the mixture with a spoon and set it aside.
6.  Dip the pastry brush in the oil, then brush the cubes of meat with the oil. Turn the cubes to coat all sides.
7.  Pour the spice-peanut mixture onto a platter. Press the cubes of meat, a few at a time, into the mixture, covering all sides. Put the cubes in the broiling pan after you cover them with the spice-peanut mixture.
8.  Put the broiling pan under the broiler for 3 minutes (set a timer if you have one).
9.  Using oven gloves or potholders, open the oven door and slide out the oven rack along with the broiler pan. Carefully stir the meat cubes with a fork to turn them over.
10. Slide the rack back and close the oven door. Broil for 2 to 3 more minutes, until the meat is no longer pink inside. Be careful to watch the meat because it may quickly burn. (Try brushing the meat with a little more oil if necessary.)

*Chichinga*

## TO SERVE:

Spoon the cubes of meat onto a serving platter. As the platter is passed around, each piece of meat may be speared with a toothpick to pick it up.

## VARIATIONS:

1. Chichinga is also made from liver or lamb as well as beef.
2. Although the version here calls for the meat to be broiled in an oven, you could also fry it in a few tablespoons of oil in a frying pan on top of a stove.
3. Older cooks might like to try broiling the meat on wooden or metal skewers. If you use wooden skewers, put them in a bowl of water to soak while you prepare the meat and seasonings. Otherwise, they might catch fire when you put them under the broiler. Soak them for about half an hour, then remove them from the water and thread several cubes of meat on each one. Be careful not to poke your fingers with the sharp point of the skewers. If the skewers are 12 inches long, you will probably have about eight skewers with pieces of meat on each one. Do not push the meat

pieces tightly together. Brush the meat on the skewers with the oil, then roll the skewers in the peanut-spice mixture. Place each skewer in the broiler pan as you coat it.

4.  You could also try barbecuing the skewers of meat.

5.  If you use skewers for the chichinga, thread a few chunks of green pepper and/or onion onto the skewers along with the meat. Peel and quarter the onion first, then separate the layers.

6.  You can vary the spiciness of the seasonings by using more or less red pepper, or black pepper or chili powder instead of or along with the red pepper.

# Fish Turnovers

These turnovers are delicious served hot or cold. In Africa, they are often sold by the roadside as a snack, or served as appetizers at parties. Our family likes them, accompanied by a salad, as a light supper dish. These turnovers are somewhat similar to the *samosas* served in Eastern or Southern Africa. However, samosas, with their Indian roots, are curry-flavored and deep-fried.

This recipe makes fifteen to seventeen turnovers.

**INGREDIENTS:**
**Filling:**
> 1 egg
> 1½ teaspoons tomato paste
> ½ cup canned tuna fish, drained
> 1 tablespoon onion, chopped
> 2 tablespoons margarine
> 2 tablespoons water
> 1 tablespoon flour
> ⅛ teaspoon salt
> a dash or two ground red pepper

**Pastry:**

  2 cups flour (plus extra for rolling out pastry)
  1 teaspoon salt
  ⅔ cup shortening
  6 to 7 tablespoons cold water

**UTENSILS:**

  small saucepan
  timer
  can opener
  paring knife
  cutting board
  small frying pan
  measuring cups
  measuring spoons
  wooden spoon
  small bowl
  large mixing bowl
  2 table knives or pastry blender
  rolling pin
  knife (or a 3-inch circle, like a jar lid, a glass, bowl,
    or biscuit cutter)
  cookie sheet
  fork
  oven gloves
  pancake turner
  wire rack

**DIRECTIONS:**

1. Assemble ingredients and utensils.
2. Put the egg in the small saucepan, cover the egg with water, and bring the water to a boil over high heat. Lower the heat to low and cook for 15 to 20 minutes (set the timer). As soon as the egg is cooked, turn off the stove, remove the egg from the water using a spoon, and run it under cold water for a minute (or carry the pan carefully to the sink, pour off the boiling water, cover the egg with cold water, and let it sit for a couple of minutes) before peeling it.

3. While the egg is cooking, open the cans of tomato paste and tuna fish.

4. Peel and chop the onion on the cutting board, then peel the egg if you haven't already.

5. Melt the margarine (or shortening) in the frying pan over medium-low heat. Add the tablespoon of chopped onion, then cook it for a couple of minutes until it is clear but not brown. Turn the heat to low. Add the water, tomato paste, flour, salt, and pepper; then stir well. Stir in the tuna fish with a wooden spoon. Cook for just a couple of minutes before turning off the heat, removing the pan from the burner, and letting it rest while you fix the pastry.

6. In a large mixing bowl, stir together the flour and salt. Using a pastry blender, two knives, or your hands, cut in the shortening until it is in pieces the size of small peas. Sprinkle 2 tablespoons of the water over part of the flour mixture, then gently push it into the side of the bowl with a fork, mixing it as you do. Continue sprinkling the water on the flour until it is all moistened. Put some flour on your hands and form the mixture into a ball. Divide the ball into

*Fish Turnovers*

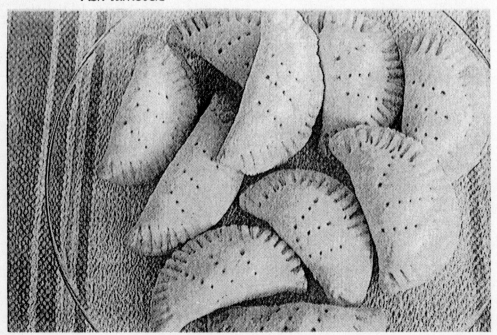

two smaller balls. Set one of the balls on a lightly floured surface, flatten the ball with your hands, then roll it out with a floured rolling pin until it is ⅛ to ¼ inch thick. If the dough is crumbly, add a little more water. If it is sticky, add a little more flour.

7. Using a lid, glass, biscuit cutter, small bowl, or a knife, cut the pastry into 3-inch squares or circles. Roll the scraps again and continue making squares or circles. When you have finished making the circles or squares, set them on the cookie sheet.

8. Turn on the oven to 400 degrees to preheat. Put half of a tablespoon of the filling in the center of each circle or square. Dip your finger into a cup of water and moisten the edges with a little water; then fold them over to form triangles or half circles (depending on whether you used squares or circles). Dip the fork in flour, then crimp around the edges of the turnover to seal it well. Prick the top of the turnover several times with a fork. Be careful not to prick through the bottom side of the turnover.

9. Bake in a hot oven (400 degrees) for about 20 minutes, until crisp and lightly golden. Set the timer for 15 minutes and check to see how they are baking.

10. While the first batch of turnovers are baking, repeat the circle/square-making process with the second ball of dough.

11. When the first batch of turnovers is done, put on oven gloves and carefully remove the cookie sheet from the oven. Younger cooks should be sure to get a grown-up assistant to help with this step.

12. Using a pancake turner, remove the turnovers from the cookie sheet onto a wire rack to cool.

13. If you have a second cookie sheet, continue from Step 7 above. If not, wait a few minutes for the cookie sheet to cool, then continue as above.

## TO SERVE:

Fish turnovers are very versatile. We often make them to take to summer picnics or eat in the car when we travel. Our children enjoy them as a refreshing change from sandwiches in their lunchboxes. They are equally popular as appetizers at parties. Finally, turnovers are wonderful for lunch or dinner, served warm from the oven with a crisp green salad.

## VARIATIONS:

These turnovers can also be made with canned corned beef or any leftover cooked fish or meat.

## HINT:

A shortcut method is to buy an already prepared pastry dough or to use a packaged pastry mix.

# Kelewele
# (Fried Plantain Cubes)

This dish has always been one of our family's favorites. We used to go for walks in the evenings in Ghana to the place where lamps and candles flickered in the night, guiding us to the women who prepared and sold evening snacks. We bought our Kelewele there, neatly wrapped in newspaper.

## INGREDIENTS:

**2 ripe plantains (yellow or yellow and black and soft)**
**water**
**½ teaspoon salt**
**½ teaspoon ground dried ginger**
**¼ teaspoon ground red pepper**
**peanut or other vegetable oil (for deep frying)**

*Kelewele with Peanuts*

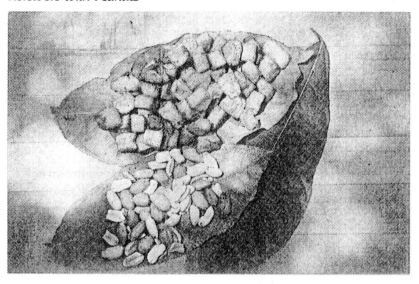

**UTENSILS:**
**knife**
**cutting board**
**bowl**
**measuring spoons**
**electric deep fryer**
**long-handled slotted spoon**
**paper towels, cloth, or brown paper**

**DIRECTIONS:**
1. Assemble the ingredients and utensils.
2. Peel the plantains and remove any of the fibrous strings (see *Plantain Chips* recipe for directions on how to peel plantains). Cut the plantain into small cubes (about ¼ to ½ inch), and put them in a bowl filled with water and the salt. After cutting all the plantain and adding it to the bowl, stir it once or twice, then drain off the water.
3. After pouring off all the water, add the ginger and red pepper. Stir the plantain cubes and spices well.

4.  Heat the oil in the electric deep fryer to 365 or 375 degrees. When it is heated, carefully use a long-handled slotted spoon or a fryer basket to fry spoonfuls of the plantain cubes at a time, turning them gently with the slotted spoon so they brown evenly. It should take about 5 to 10 minutes.
5.  When the cubes are golden brown, lift them out carefully and drain on paper towels, cloth, or brown paper.

**TO SERVE:**

Kelewele may be served warm or at room temperature. It is especially good when served with roasted unsalted peanuts.

**VARIATIONS:**
1.  When ripe plantains are sliced (rather than cubed) and fried or roasted without the spices, they make a wonderful accompaniment to stews, such as *Bean Stew*. See the recipes for *Fried Red Plantain Slices* and *Roasted Ripe Plantain.*
2.  Older cooks may like to try grinding a little peeled fresh ginger and washed fresh chili pepper (about an inch of each) with a tablespoon of water in a blender or food processor; then use it to replace the dried ginger and pepper in the recipe.

# Fresh Coconut

Most people have probably tasted coconut, but it wasn't until I went to Africa that I saw fresh coconuts opened. There are two kinds of coconuts—the green fresh ones and the brown hard ones we find in our grocery stores. One day, when we visited one of my husband's uncles, he sent someone out to pick two coconuts for us. The green top was chopped off and we drank the refreshing liquid right from the coconut, then we ate the soft milky inside with spoons.

My favorite way to eat coconut is the way children in Ghana do—as a snack. It is very rich, and should be saved for a special treat. It is amazing how good it tastes without any sugar added to it.

Whenever I buy a fresh coconut in the store, I always shake several of them and buy the one that feels like it has the most liquid inside. I have heard that there are two ways to open

*Fresh Coconut*

a coconut—a fast way and a slow way. Because we are always in a hurry, I can tell you that the fast way works for me; but I will also describe the slow way for those of you who are more patient.

**INGREDIENTS:**
fresh coconut(s)

**UTENSILS:**
newspapers
hammer
ice pick, chisel, or small screwdriver
glass or cup
vegetable peeler
table knife
plate
tea strainer
(It also helps to have strong arms!)

**DIRECTIONS:**
1. It is best to crack open coconuts on a hard surface—like a cement or linoleum floor. We usually open ours in the garage, but you can do it inside a room too.
2. Spread several newspapers on the floor under the coconut. Look at the coconut and find the three dark spots near one end. These spots are called the "eyes" of the coconut. Hold the ice pick (or screwdriver) against one of the eyes of the coconut and hit it several times with the hammer, until it goes into the coconut and makes a hole. Be careful not to hit your fingers! Pull out the ice pick and do the same thing at another eye.
3. After you remove the ice pick, set the tea strainer over the glass, then turn the coconut upside down over the glass and let the liquid from the coconut drip into the glass. The strainer will keep the brown flakes out of the liquid (If you want the juice to come out faster, make a third hole at the third eye of the coconut). When the liquid has dripped out, move the glass away to a safe place, like a table or

countertop. In our family, everyone wants to be the first to get to drink the milky liquid from inside the coconut. When I can get it away, I like to pour it into tropical fruit salads, but it usually disappears by the time we have the coconut open. The fresher the coconut, the better the liquid tastes.

4. Now you are ready to crack the coconut. While one person is cracking the coconut, everyone else should stand well away from pieces of flying coconut shell. (We have never had any problems—and children as young as three years old have helped us—but we have always been careful to have a grown-up supervising and ready to finish up after the initial cracking open of the coconut.) It may take several people hitting the coconut in the center with a hammer several times before the shell cracks open.

5. Smaller pieces of shell can be hit with the white coconut meat facing the newspaper. When the shell breaks, sometimes the coconut meat pops away from the shell in big chunks, and sometimes it has to be carefully pried off with the knife. This is not really hard; it just takes a little practice. By the way, when you open the coconut, you should not find mold on the coconut meat—either the brown side or the white side. If there is mold, the coconut will probably taste rancid, and you should take it back to the store where you bought it and complain. To be on the safe side, you might want to buy two coconuts.

6. Once you have separated the coconut meat from the shell, you can cut away the brown skin on the meat with the vegetable peeler or knife. Be careful peeling because the coconut is oily and can be slippery. After peeling the coconut, rinse it off with cool water and cut it into small chunks.

**TO SERVE:**

Place the fresh coconut chunks on a plate, then eat and enjoy yourself! You have earned it. You could also serve some hot corn along with it (see the recipes for boiled or roasted corn).

**VARIATIONS:**

1.  The slow way to open a coconut is the same at the beginning, but after you drain the liquid from the coconut eyes, you put the coconut on a cookie sheet or in a baking dish in a preheated oven (turn the oven on to 350 degrees to preheat before you take out the liquid in the coconut) for 45 minutes to an hour. When the shell begins to crack, remove it from the oven, let it cool enough to handle, pry off any shell that still remains, and peel it with the vegetable peeler.

2.  For directions on how to make coconut milk, see the recipe for *Rice and Beans*.

# Akla
# (Bean Balls)

Akla is just one name for these yummy relatives of our Southern hush puppies. Akla are made from black-eyed peas, not cornmeal. I have seen them called bean balls, bean cakes, cowpea paste fritters, fried cowpea balls, akara, accara, kosai, kose, and koose. Whatever name you use, they are a popular African snack food, breakfast food, or supper dish. The hardest (and slowest) part of making Bean Balls is getting the paste ready, but the balls are worth the work!

This recipe makes about three dozen bean balls.

**INGREDIENTS:**

1 cup dried black-eyed peas (cowpeas)
water
2 tablespoons minced onion
½ teaspoon ground ginger (or 2 teaspoons fresh minced ginger)
oil or shortening for deep frying
½ teaspoon salt
⅛ teaspoon ground red pepper (or more if you like)

**UTENSILS:**
   large mixing bowl (stainless steel is good)
   electric blender
   measuring spoons
   measuring cup
   wooden mixing spoon
   small mixing bowl
   paring knife
   cutting board
   electric deep fryer with wire basket or slotted spoon
   electric mixer or hand mixer
   spoon
   timer
   long-handled wooden spoon
   colander

**DIRECTIONS:**

1. Assemble the ingredients and utensils.

2. Pick through the beans and take out any stones or yucky-looking beans. Put the beans in the large bowl, rinse them with cool water, then fill the bowl with water. Using both hands, rub the beans together between your palms. The skins of the beans (the "seed coats") will come off. This is called "dehulling." As the skins come off, they will float to the top of the water, and the beans (their fancy name is "cotyledons") will sink to the bottom. The skins can be scooped off or poured off, or you can add more water until they float over the edge of the bowl. Keep working at this until all (or almost all) of the skins are off. It may take one person half an hour or longer. Don't worry if the beans break into pieces. Also, the longer the beans soak in the water, the bigger they get. For bean balls, it is better not to let them soak for a long time.

3. When you finish dehulling the beans, put part of them in an electric blender with a few tablespoons of clean water. Blend them until you have a smooth paste. Continue grinding the beans, and adding water (up to ½ cup) until you have a smooth paste. If the blender gets jammed easily, do the beans in two or three batches, and empty them into a small bowl as each batch is ground. Grinding the beans only takes a few minutes. Sometimes you may need to unplug the blender and push the paste down the sides with a spoon to get it all mixed.

4. Now you are ready to make the balls. Peel and finely chop (mince) the onion. Do the same thing with the ginger—if you are using fresh ginger. Set them aside.

5. Put the oil or shortening into the electric fryer and plug it in to heat up.

6. Using the electric mixer (or a hand rotary mixer), mix the paste for 3 minutes. Add a couple of tablespoons of water if it seems too thick. This step is important because it gets air into the batter to make the fried balls light.

7. Just before frying, sprinkle the onion, ginger, red pepper, and salt over the mixture and gently stir them in with a spoon.

8. Carefully drop the batter by spoonfuls (about a heaping teaspoonful) into the hot oil, and fry for about 3 minutes. If the balls sink down to the bottom of the fryer, the oil is not hot enough. If they brown too quickly, so the insides don't have time to cook, the oil is too hot. Be very careful when adding the bean paste. If you hold the spoon too high, the hot oil might splatter you when it drops in; if too low, you might burn your fingers by accident. Younger cooks should definitely have a grown-up assistant for this step. Also, curious cooks should not get their faces too close to the bubbling oil in case of any unexpected splatters.

9. Fry in small batches until all the batter is used up. The balls should be turned over once with a long-handled wooden spoon halfway through the cooking time, so they are evenly cooked. They are done when they are golden brown and crisp. Lift the wire basket up or use a slotted spoon to remove the balls from the oil. Drain in a colander, bowl, or on paper towels.

**TO SERVE:**

Akla makes a nice vegetarian party appetizer. They can be eaten alone or served on a platter with toothpicks and a bowl of peppery sauce. Either way, you will enjoy these bean balls!

**VARIATIONS:**

1. Substitute a piece of fresh chili pepper for the ground red pepper, and add it to the blender when you grind the beans.

2. Deep fry the balls in two inches of oil in a heavy, 2-quart saucepan.

3. Add an egg when you grind the beans and use less water.

4. Omit the red pepper.

# Plantain Chips

A few weeks ago, I helped one of my daughters fix these at a multi-cultural fair at her junior high school. Very quickly word spread throughout the gym that these were great, and we were surrounded by a crowd that could barely wait until we lifted the fryer basket. Kids who had hardly wanted to sample their first chip came back with their friends and their friends' friends. Anyone who likes potato chips is likely to enjoy plantain chips. They are not at all sweet like chips made from ripe bananas.

**INGREDIENTS:**

> 2 to 3 large green plantains
> oil for deep frying
> salt

**UTENSILS:**

> electric deep fryer with basket or slotted spoon
> cutting board
> paring knife
> grater
> paper towels or cloth

**DIRECTIONS:**

1. Assemble ingredients and utensils.
2. Peel one plantain. To do this, slice each end off, then make three cuts around the circumference through the peel, but not through the plantain itself: one at the center and one about an inch from each end. Finally, make a cut the length of the plantain. Put the tip of the knife into the long cut and pry the peel loose to get it started. If it is difficult to peel, find an adult helper.
3. With one hand, hold the grater against you, so the grater is horizontal over the cutting board. Hold the peeled plantain in the other hand, so it is perpendicular to the grater; then grate it on the wide "shred" blade into thin rounds or ovals.

This takes a little practice to get the pressure just right. Cut the plantain in half first if that is easier to get it started.

4. Heat the oil in an electric deep fryer to about 365 degrees, and fry the chips in batches without crowding them, until they are crisp and golden. The trick to frying the chips is to gently drop the slices into the oil one at a time. If you throw them all in, drop them too hard, or get your fingers too close to the oil, you will burn yourself. If you pour in a cupful of slices, they will clump together and not cook as separate chips. Stir the chips with a long-handled wooden or slotted spoon while they are frying. They will only take a few minutes to fry, depending on how thinly they are sliced or grated, how many you cook at once, and how hot the oil is.

5. Remove the fry basket or use the slotted spoon to remove the chips when they are done. Drain them on paper towels or clean cloths.

6. Salt the chips lightly while they are still warm.

7. Repeat steps one through eight with the other plantain(s).

*Plantain Chips*

**TO SERVE:**

Plantain Chips may be served as a side dish with a main meal, or they are always a hit when served as an appetizer or party snack. Eat and enjoy them! We always cook these the same day we plan to eat them, but if there are any left over, store them in an airtight container.

**VARIATIONS:**

Use an electric fry pan instead of a deep fryer.

# Avocado Spread

The first time someone offered me a "pear" in Ghana, I was surprised to bite into an avocado! I did not know that avocados are known as "avocado pears" in Ghana—or simply "pears" for short. This mashed avocado spread is a nice change from butter or margarine on toast, and is a great way to start the day—especially when accompanied by fresh squeezed orange juice and lemongrass tea.

This recipe serves four to six people.

**INGREDIENTS:**

2 ripe avocados
½ lime (or 1 teaspoon lime juice)
⅛ teaspoon salt
2 or 3 dashes ground red pepper

**UTENSILS:**

cutting knife
bowl
fork
measuring spoons

**DIRECTIONS:**

1. Assemble ingredients and utensils.
2. Cut the avocados in half and remove the seeds from the centers.
3. Peel off the green skin and put the avocado halves in the bowl.
4. Mash the avocado with a fork.
5. Squeeze the lime half to get 1 teaspoon of lime juice, then add it to the avocado, along with the salt and 2 shakes of red pepper. Mix well with the fork and taste. Add another dash of red pepper if you like.

**TO SERVE:**

Spread on toast, bread, or crackers for breakfast, lunch, or as a party appetizer.

**VARIATIONS:**

Use lemon juice instead of lime juice.

*Avocado Spread*

# Groundnut Paste

In Ghana, nobody would probably know what you wanted if you asked for some peanut butter. Instead, you would have to ask for "groundnut paste" because peanuts are called "groundnuts" in Ghana or, in the Twi language, *nkate*. If you have a food processor or blender, you can make your own peanut spread (or groundnut paste).

*Groundnut Paste*

## INGREDIENTS:

1 cup unsalted dry roasted peanuts
⅛ teaspoon salt
2 tablespoons water
1 tablespoon peanut oil (optional)

## UTENSILS:

measuring cup
measuring spoon
food processor or blender
bowl
spoon or fork

## DIRECTIONS:

1. Assemble ingredients and utensils.
2. Put the cup of peanuts, the ⅛ tablespoon of salt, two tablespoons of water, and the tablespoon of peanut oil (if you like) in the food processor and grind them together. If you use an electric food blender, first grind the cup of peanuts ¼ cup at a time. Pour the ground peanuts into a bowl and add ⅛ teaspoon salt, 1 tablespoon peanut oil, and 2 tablespoons of water. Mix this together well with a spoon or fork, and add more oil or water if it seems too dry and crumbly.

## TO SERVE:

Groundnut paste is delicious on crackers, bread, or toast, with or without papaya jam.

## VARIATIONS:

You could simply buy some natural-style peanut butter with no sugar added. Groundnut paste is unsweetened and somehow thicker than American-style peanut butter, and it tastes more "peanutty."

# Papaya Jam
# (Pawpaw Jam)

Here is something that I'll bet you haven't had before. In Ghana, you don't find grapes and strawberries and blueberries and apples and blackberries, so people make jams from the fruits that they do have—papayas and mangoes and pineapples and oranges. Although the fruit may be different, the sweet taste and texture are familiar.

**INGREDIENTS:**

    **1 papaya, almost ripe (2 cups chopped papaya)**
    **½ cup sugar**
    **1 cup water**
    **1½-inch piece of fresh ginger (2 teaspoons fresh**
    **minced ginger)**
    **water**

**UTENSILS:**

    **small saucepan with lid**
    **paring knife**
    **measuring cups**
    **measuring spoons**
    **cutting board**
    **small spoon**
    **wooden spoon**
    **timer**

**DIRECTIONS:**

1. Assemble ingredients and utensils.
2. Rinse the papaya under cold water, cut it in half, and scoop out the seeds with a spoon. Cut off the peel, then chop the papaya on the cutting board to get about 2 cups of papaya cubes. Put it into the saucepan.
3. Cut the peel off of the ginger, and mince it into tiny pieces. Add 2 teaspoons of the minced ginger to the saucepan.
4. Add the cup of water and ½ cup sugar to the saucepan.

5. Put the saucepan on the stove, turn the heat to high, and stir the mixture until the sugar dissolves and the water comes to a boil.
6. Lower the heat to simmer, stir the mixture well, then cover the pan. Let the fruit mixture simmer for 1½ to 2 hours, stirring well every 15 minutes. (Set a timer every 15 minutes to remind you.) This is the hard part because you have to keep checking that there is enough water to keep the jam from sticking and burning. We usually have to add about ¼ cup of water every half hour or so. When the jam looks done (all the fruit will cook down into little pieces), turn off the heat and let the pan cool. Put the jam into a jar and store it covered in the refrigerator.

## TO SERVE:

This jam spread is delicious—whether on toast at breakfast, in sandwiches at lunch, or on crackers as a snack or party food.

## VARIATIONS:

1. Instead of papaya, use pineapple or green or ripe mango.
2. Only cook the fruit for 15 minutes, then serve it as stewed fruit or a fruit sauce over ice cream or frozen yogurt.

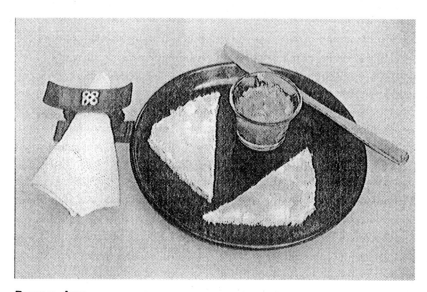

*Papaya Jam*

# Desserts and Sweets

# Pawpaw with Lime

Our family first learned to enjoy pawpaw with lime for breakfast when we lived in Ghana, where we could go outside and pick the fruit just before eating it. In Pennsylvania, the imported fruit costs more, so we serve it with lime mainly as a light dessert on special occasions. We all agree that there is something about the flavor of ripe papaya and lime together that makes this combination taste extra nice.

This recipe serves two people.

**INGREDIENTS:**

**one ripe papaya**
**½ small lime**

**UTENSILS:**

**cutting board**
**knife**
**spoon**
**2 small serving plates**

**DIRECTIONS:**
1. Wash the papaya and lime under cool water. Always be gentle, so you don't bruise the papaya.
2. Use the knife to cut the papaya in half lengthwise on the cutting board.
3. Use the spoon to carefully scoop out the seeds.
4. Cut the lime in half, and cut one half into 2 pieces. Save the other half for another time.

**TO SERVE:**

Arrange one half of the papaya on each plate and set the piece of lime next to it. Squeeze the lime over the papaya, then scoop up the papaya with a spoon the way you would eat a melon.

**VARIATIONS:**

1. If you want to serve this as an appetizer or at the beginning of a meal, you could cut the papaya into four smaller pieces and the lime into four wedges to serve four people.

2. If you have bad luck and get a slightly under-ripe papaya, you could try sprinkling it with sugar before eating it.

# Twisted Cakes

Twisted Cakes are called *Chinchin* in Nigeria and *Atwemo* in Ghana. These crisp, slightly sweet "cookies" (which are called biscuits in Ghana) are often eaten at celebrations such as Christmas or at parties in Ghana; and they are sold by street vendors in Nigeria. They are also fun to make.

This is a wonderful recipe for assembly-line production—especially if an adult is present to fry them as kids roll out the dough, cut it into diamonds, and pull the slits through. Even the smallest helper can carry plates of twisted dough to the fryer or loosen the cut diamonds from the board or waxed paper so they can be twisted.

## INGREDIENTS:
**4 cups flour**
**½ teaspoon salt**
**2 teaspoons baking powder**
**½ cup butter or margarine**
**½ cup sugar**
**½ teaspoon ground nutmeg**
**1 egg**
**¾ cup milk**
**1 teaspoon vanilla flavoring**
**vegetable oil for deep frying**

## UTENSILS:
**measuring cups**
**large bowl**
**flour sifter**
**pastry cutter (optional)**
**measuring spoons**
**mixing spoon**
**small bowl**
**fork**
**waxed paper or board**
**rolling pin**
**knife**
**2 plates**
**electric deep fryer**
**colander or paper towels**
**long-handled slotted spoon**

## DIRECTIONS:
1. Assemble ingredients and utensils.
2. Sift flour, salt, and baking powder together in a large bowl.
3. Use a pastry blender or your hands to rub or cut the butter into the sifted ingredients in the large bowl.
4. Add the sugar and nutmeg, then mix with a spoon.

5. In the small bowl, beat the egg with a fork, then add the milk and vanilla.
6. Add the liquid ingredients to the flour mixture and mix well (your hands work better than a spoon) into a stiff dough.
7. Divide the dough into four equal parts. Roll one part of the dough out on a lightly floured board or piece of waxed paper until it is about ¼ inch thick.
8. Cut the dough into strips about ½ inch wide and 1 inch or so long, with slanted ends to make diamond shapes. With a knife, make a small slit in the middle. Twist by pulling one corner all the way through the slit. (See the pictures below.) Put the uncooked cakes on plates and continue rolling out the uncooked portions of dough, saving and rerolling all the scraps.

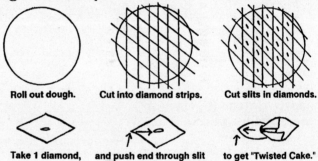

Roll out dough.  Cut into diamond strips.  Cut slits in diamonds.

Take 1 diamond,  and push end through slit  to get "Twisted Cake."

9. Fry the cookies. Younger cooks should have an adult assist with the frying, and older cooks should have supervision when frying the cakes. Heat the oil in a small electric deep fryer, and fry about a dozen of the twisted cakes at a time, turning them once to brown evenly. They cook quickly. When they are golden and crisp, lift them out of the oil with a fryer basket or long-handled slotted spoon. Drain them on paper towels or in a colander.

**TO SERVE:**

Twisted cakes, or *Atwemo*, are great by themselves as a snack or with ice cream or fruit for dessert. They can be stored in an airtight container, and they also freeze well. Even children who are hesitant to try strange new foods seem to love these.

*Twisted Cakes*

## VARIATIONS:

1.  Instead of nutmeg, substitute grated orange rind, caraway seed, or aniseed.
2.  Leave out the vanilla flavoring.
3.  For younger cooks or older cooks in a hurry, simply cut the dough into simple shapes like triangles, and fry them without slitting and twisting them. You can also do this to use up the scraps of dough left over.
4.  The trick to making twisted cakes is to pull one end all the way through the slit, pulling that end inside-out. When our children were young, they sometimes just tucked the end through the slit without pulling it all the way through. After the cakes were fried, they were delighted to discover that they had created bird shapes. Look carefully at the photograph to see if you can find some of the "birds" among the twisted cakes.

*Desserts and Sweets*                    137

# Tropical Fruit Salad

This is probably my personal all-time favorite choice for a Ghanaian dessert—whether it be for just family or a fancy dinner party. When it is accompanied by *Twisted Cakes,* it is hard to beat.

Some people think it tastes best if you make it right before you eat it, so you can taste the flavor of each individual fruit. Other people like to make it a few hours ahead, so the fruit flavors have a chance to blend together. Whichever way you choose, the best part is that the exact fruits you use and their proportions are not really all that important. You can change it to suit your mood and the fruit you like and can easily find. The secret is to find ripe, fresh fruit and cut all the pieces to be about the same size.

*Tropical Fruit Salad*

Years ago, we always had to buy a whole pineapple or watermelon to get the fruit, which meant we either ate the salad for several days or only served it for a big party. Nowadays, many grocery stores sell already peeled and cored pineapples (much easier!) or slices of watermelon (much cheaper!). Even better are the salad bars in supermarkets that often have the more common tropical fruits already cut up, so you can buy just what you want in the exact amount.

This is the basic recipe we use for five people.

## INGREDIENTS:

> **1 small ripe papaya (1 cup diced papaya)**
> **2 medium seedless navel oranges**
> **2 cups pineapple, diced**
> **2 cups diced watermelon**
> **1 coconut (½ cup coconut juice and ¼ cup thinly sliced fresh coconut)**
> **2 medium ripe bananas**

## UTENSILS:

> **cutting board**
> **knife**
> **spoon**
> **measuring cups**
> **newspapers, hammer and small screwdriver or ice pick**
> **cup**
> **large bowl**

## DIRECTIONS:

1. Assemble ingredients and utensils.
2. Rinse the papaya with cold water, cut it in half, and use a spoon to scoop out the seeds in the center. Cut the papaya into sections, then use the knife to cut off the peel. Dice the fruit into small cubes a little less than ½ inch in size, until you have 1 cup. Put the cubes into the large bowl.
3. Rinse the oranges, peel them, and break the sections apart. Cut each section into three or four pieces (put several sections together to cut them at the same time). Add the orange pieces to the bowl.

4. Cut the peeled, cored pineapple into small cubes, then add 2 cups of the pineapple cubes to the bowl.
5. Remove any seeds from the watermelon and cut it into small pieces. Add 2 cups of watermelon chunks to the bowl.
6. Crack open the coconut and peel it, saving the juice (see the recipe for *Fresh Coconut* for directions on preparing a coconut). Taste the juice to make sure that it is sweet, then add ½ cup to the bowl.
7. Slice ½ cup of the coconut and add it to the salad. Stir well.

**TO SERVE:**

Just before serving, peel the bananas, slice them lengthwise into two long pieces, then cut each piece in half lenthwise again. Chop the four long pieces into slices a little less than ½ inch long. Stir the chopped banana into the fruit salad.

Serve the fruit salad as it is in small bowls, or serve it with *Twisted Cakes,* or offer small pitchers of evaporated milk or cream at the table to pour on top (do not do this before serving or the milk or cream will curdle). You could also top each individual bowl with a spoonful of whipped cream, ice cream, or fresh or frozen yogurt. Whatever way you choose, enjoy the fresh, tropical taste!

**VARIATIONS:**

1. Use canned mandarin oranges instead of fresh oranges.
2. Use ripe mango instead of or along with the other fruits.
3. Omit the coconut and juice.
4. Squeeze fresh lime over the salad (and add a teaspoon or two of sugar if necessary).
5. For a party, buy a whole pineapple and get help to cut it in half lengthwise and remove the fruit and core without cutting the outside, so you can use the pineapple shell as a basket with the fruit salad heaped up inside. For a larger party, try using a watermelon the same way (you can even try cutting a handle for the watermelon basket).

6. Cut the bananas ahead of time, sprinkle them with lemon or lime juice to keep them from turning brown, then add them to the salad. Add a little sugar to cut the sharpness of the lemon or lime.
7. If the fruits are not naturally sweet, add a couple teaspoons of sugar to the salad to bring out their flavor.
8. Substitute cantaloupe for the papaya.
9. Substitute peeled fresh ripe peaches for the papaya, and add them with the bananas just before serving.
10. Cut the fruit several hours ahead of time (but not the bananas!), and store them separately in plastic containers in the refrigerator. Mix the different fruits together just before serving.

# Orange Slices

Often only one or two main meals are eaten daily in Ghana, along with many small snacks throughout the day. The major meals tend to be very filling and heavy, so a rich, heavy dessert after them would just be too much. Instead, people who eat dessert prefer a light fresh fruit dessert, such as orange slices. We have served orange slices to distinguished international visitors as well as family and friends. Sometimes "less" really is "more." There are two ways to prepare the oranges—either as slices or as wedges.

**INGREDIENTS:**

**1 ripe seedless navel orange per person**
**mint leaves for decoration (optional)**

**UTENSILS:**

**cutting board**
**paring knife**
**serving platter or individual dessert plates**

*Orange Slices*

## DIRECTIONS:

1. Wash the oranges, cut the ends off, and cut each orange into about four slices. Cut each slice in half.
2. Arrange orange slices on a serving platter or individual dessert plates (see drawing).

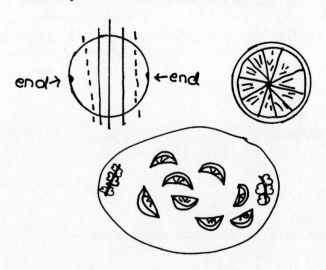

A GOOD SOUP ATTRACTS CHAIRS

## TO SERVE:

If you like, decorate the platter or plates of orange slices with clean fresh mint leaves. To eat the slices, no knives or spoons or forks are necessary! Although orange slices are a fitting ending to an African lunch or dinner, they fit in just as well at the beginning of the day, at breakfast, or in the mid-morning, afternoon, or late evening as a satisfying snack.

## VARIATIONS:

Some oranges in Ghana are very sweet, but have many seeds and tough membranes or "skin" in the center. To serve this type of orange, it is better to cut each washed orange in half through the ends first, then cut each half into three wedges (see drawing).

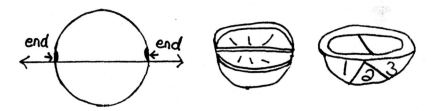

Holding a wedge tilted up against the cutting board, use a sawing motion to cut off a thin strip of the membrane along the top of the wedge (see drawing). If the oranges do not have seeds or a tough membrane, there is really no need to cut the strip off of the top of each wedge.

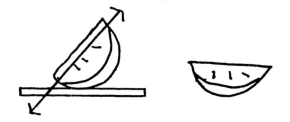

*Desserts and Sweets*

Remove any seeds, then set the wedge down with the peel against the cutting board, and make a ½-inch cut along each end to loosen the orange from the inside of the peel (see drawing).

To eat the wedges, you hold one with both hands, push down slightly on the peel ends with your thumbs, and the orange comes neatly off. This may sound complicated, but after you have done it once, it isn't hard at all. If your oranges are fresh and sweet, this dessert is truly and surprisingly elegant.

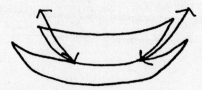

# African Doughnuts

When I was a teacher in a little town along the coast of Ghana, I would often go or send someone between classes to a house near the school where a woman sat outside in the mornings freshly frying a tasty kind of African doughnut called *togbei*. It was wonderfully satisfying with tea for breakfast or a midmorning snack. Togbei is usually made with palm wine, which is not available in the United States. Although people sometimes substitute yeast for the palm wine, our family uses a simplified version of a cake doughnut recipe. These African doughnuts are similar to the doughnut "holes" that have become popular in recent years.

The trick in making these doughnuts is to get the batter to slide smoothly off the spoon and into the oil in nice round balls without splattering and burning you. Depending on the size of the balls, this recipe will make about three dozen.

A GOOD SOUP ATTRACTS CHAIRS

**INGREDIENTS:**

shortening or oil for deep frying
1¾ cups flour
2 teaspoons baking powder
½ teaspoon grated nutmeg
½ teaspoon salt
1 egg
½ cup milk
½ cup sugar
1 tablespoon vegetable oil

**UTENSILS:**

electric deep fryer
sifter
measuring cups
measuring spoons
2 mixing bowls
fork
mixing spoon
2 dessert spoons
long-handled slotted spoon
paper towels or clean cloth
serving plate or bowl

**DIRECTIONS:**

1. Assemble ingredients and utensils.
2. Put the oil or shortening into the electric fryer, then plug it in to preheat. Get an adult helper to make sure that the fryer will heat to about 375 degrees and it is not too full of oil or shortening. (With a fryer basket, the fryer should be about half filled; without a fryer basket, up to two-thirds full. If there is too much oil when you put the doughnuts in to fry, it will bubble up over the sides.)
3. In one mixing bowl, sift together the flour, baking powder, nutmeg, and salt. Set the bowl aside.
4. Break the egg into another mixing bowl, beat it with a fork, then add the milk, sugar, and oil. Mix well.
5. Gradually stir the flour mixture into the liquid mixture.

6. Dip the dessert spoons into the hot oil, then scoop up a small spoonful of batter with one spoon and use the second small spoon to slide it off the first spoon into the oil. (Be careful not to get too close to the oil, or you will burn your fingers. Also, be careful not to be too high above the oil, or the balls will splatter and burn you!) Younger cooks should definitely ask an older, more experienced cook to help out.

7. Repeat Step 6 until there are six or so balls frying. Each ball will quickly float up to the surface, and most of them will turn themselves over after about a minute. If they don't turn over, use a wooden or slotted spoon to turn them over, and let them fry until both sides are golden brown. It will just take a minute or two. As the balls finish frying, lift them up over the oil with a slotted spoon, let the extra oil drip back into the fryer for a few seconds, then put them on a clean cloth or paper towels to absorb the extra oil.

8. Repeat the frying process until all of the batter is used. You may need to add a little more oil or shortening if the level lowers while you are frying. If you do, wait about 5 minutes for the oil to heat up again before you continue frying.

## TO SERVE:

Enjoy these doughnuts in the morning for breakfast, any-time for a snack, or serve them at the end of a meal for dessert. We eat them after cooking them—as soon as they cool.

## VARIATIONS:

1. Add ½ teaspoon vanilla when you add the milk.
2. Use melted butter or margarine instead of salad oil.
3. Use ¼ teaspoon nutmeg and ¼ teaspoon cinnamon.
4. Use evaporated milk instead of regular milk.

# Groundnut Toffee (or Peanut Cakes)

When I taught school in Ghana, my husband's sister Eunice, or Afua, came to live with me and attend the school. She was an enterprising young girl, and one of the first things she did was make a kind of toffee, or candy, to sell to her fellow students. This is a simple, easy-to-make toffee that is popular with kids everywhere.

## INGREDIENTS:

    ¾ cup peanuts
    ½ cup sugar
    2 tablespoons water

## UTENSILS:

    measuring cups
    rolling pin
    waxed paper
    cutting board
    measuring spoons
    2-quart saucepan
    wooden spoon
    spatula, knife, or spoon

**DIRECTIONS:**

1. Crush the peanuts with a rolling pin on a piece of waxed paper. The crushed peanuts can be as fine or as coarse as you like. Set them aside.
2. Wet a cutting board with a little water and set it aside.
3. Put the water and sugar in the saucepan on the stove, then turn the burner on to medium. Heat the water and sugar

*Groundnut Toffee*

**A GOOD SOUP ATTRACTS CHAIRS**

mixture, stirring a little until the sugar dissolves (it will become clear). Continue cooking on medium without stirring until the mixture, or toffee, turns brown. It will probably take 10 to 15 minutes. Turn the pan a few times if it seems to be browning unevenly. (It is important to watch carefully when the mixture begins to brown, so it doesn't burn and become charcoal.) When it is a nice golden brown, quickly stir in the nuts and remove the pan from the heat. Don't forget to turn off the stove.

4. Pour the toffee onto the wet cutting board, and use the spatula, knife, or spoon to press the toffee flat. (It will be very hot, so be careful not to burn your fingers.) Wet the spatula with hot water or put a little margarine on it if it gets sticky.

## TO SERVE:

As the toffee cools, it gets hard, so you can either break it into pieces, or use a sharp knife to mark squares off that will break evenly when it is cool. Keep the uneaten portion (if there is any!) in an airtight plastic container or a metal tin.

## VARIATIONS:

1. Instead of using a wet cutting board, grease a pan with a little margarine or butter and use a buttered spatula to press the toffee mixture into the pan to cool.

2. Instead of making the toffee into squares or pieces, roll it into small balls as it cools.

3. Toast ¾ cup dried unsweetened coconut on a cookie sheet in a preheated 350-degree oven for just a few minutes. (It will probably brown in less than 5 minutes.) Substitute the coconut for the broken peanuts in the recipe to make *Coconut Toffee*.

# How to Have an African Party

Now that you know something about West African cooking, why not give an African party? Here are some ideas to get you started:

First, decide how many people you want to invite, so you can plan the menu. Between eight and twelve people is a nice number for a party, but you can invite as few as two or as many as you have room for.

## FOOD:

Decide on a beverage or two to serve. *Ginger Beer* or one of the squashes is nice; but if time is a problem, you could also serve lemonade or limeade made from frozen concentrate or ginger ale. For a small number of people, you might decide simply to have an afternoon tea party with *Lemongrass Tea*— then you would only need something to serve with the tea.

Plan a few appetizers—like peanuts or *Plantain Chips* or *Chichinga* (beef kebobs).

If you want to have a meal, decide on a main dish that is easy to serve—like *Jollof Rice* or *Peanut Butter Stew* with rice and condiments.

Decide whether or not to serve any side dishes, like *Kelewele* or corn.

Finally, choose a dessert. *Twisted Cakes* go well with *Tropical Fruit Salad,* and the fruit salad looks very festive when served in a watermelon or pineapple basket.

If you are having a big party, make sure you start planning a couple of weeks ahead. Once you have your menu, make a grocery list, and see if there are any ingredients that may be hard to find at the last minute. For example, if you want to cook *Kelewele,* you must buy green plantain ahead of time, so it has time to ripen before the party. Shop at least a couple of days before the party. Figure out whether there is anything you could cook ahead of time and freeze, like *Twisted Cakes.* Make a beverage like *Ginger Beer* or *Lemon Squash* a few days ahead of time (you can freeze that too). The more organized you are, the more fun you will have the day of the party. Let your parents and friends help.

### INVITATIONS:

You can invite your friends personally or over the telephone; but sending or giving out invitations can be fun too.

Colors that often represent Africa are red, green, and yellow. You might use these colors on your invitation. When my children were younger and we had people over for dinner and served these recipes, the children sometimes drew pictures of the flag of Ghana on the front of homemade menus. It is a black star on a yellow stripe, with a red stripe along the top and a green stripe along the bottom. Masi labeled our house "The Ghana Chop Bar" (*chop* means "to eat," and a *chop bar* is an informal or roadside restaurant). Abena drew morning glories. You could draw a picture of the map of Africa, or of any African flag you like. You could also just use the words "Come" or "You're Invited." Use your imagination!

Tell your friends when and where and what time the party will be and tell them it is an African party. If you will serve dinner, let them know; and if you want them to tell you if they are coming, write "R.S.V.P." and your phone number on the invitation. R.S.V.P. stands for the French words, *respondez s'il vous plait,* which translates to "reply if it pleases you." My husband says that when he was a child, he and his friends thought that it stood for "rice stew very plenty."

### DECORATIONS:

Go tropical. If your party is in the summertime, it can be outside. That would be nice. If you live in a colder climate or it is cold outside, create a mood of warmth and friendliness by using lots of color and greenery—like ferns and houseplants, or bamboo or even tall freshly cut corn stalks. Put a bright-colored batiked or tie-dyed cloth on the table, and use colored napkins. A centerpiece of a potted plant—like flowering hibiscus—is nice, or use a vase of marigolds, or bouganvillea, or whatever you like. Just make sure that the flowers are colorful. Some people decorate with fresh fruits and vegetables. They might put bunches of bananas or coconuts or pineapples around the room to make it feel more African. Create your own ideas.

## MUSIC:

To make the party a success, get authentic African music. Because "Afropop" music is hugely popular now, it is not difficult to find. If you do not have a library or record shop nearby, call or write your local National Public Radio station to find out if and when they broadcast the program "Afropop Worldwide." Even if they do not, you can write for the listener's guide, which is filled with helpful information about music resources, different groups, the types of music they play, and recording labels. Include a self-addressed business-size envelope (9½ inches or 24.1 cm long) and four first class stamps with your request, and mail it to:

AFROPOP WORLDWIDE
Listener's Guide
National Public Radio
2025 M St. NW
Washington, D.C. 20036

A popular group from Ghana is the African Brothers Band. Ghana is also famous for its many "highlife" bands. A well-known Nigerian (Nigeria is also in West Africa) drummer and singer is Olatunji. Other popular Nigerians include King Sunny Ade or Fela Kuti. Tabu Ley-Rochereau is from Zaire, and Youssou N'Dour is from Senegal. Of course, Paul Simon made South African music familiar with his album *Graceland*, and Ladysmith Black Mambazo, who performed on that album, has released many recordings that are available in the United States. Two other South Africans, trumpet player Hugh Masekela and singer Miriam Makeba, have been known in the U.S. for decades. Hugh Masekela also wrote music for the popular musical *Sarafina!*

Depending on the age of your guests, you may or may not want to dance. Again, you decide. African music is easy to dance to. As my husband's aunt once told me, "dancing is letting the music move your feet." If you just want the music to add to the festive mood, that is fine too.

## GAMES:

Not everyone wants to dance, but there are lots of games you can play. A famous board game in Ghana is called *Oware*. Another name for it might be "Capture the Seeds." I have seen third graders play it enthusiastically, as well as teenagers and adults. It is usually played with small stones or seeds on a board with twelve little cups—two rows of six cups each. Sometimes people substitute egg cartons for the wooden boards. In Rwanda, it is known as *Igisoro*, and people just dig twelve small holes in the ground for the board. The same basic game is known as *Ayo* in Nigeria, *Mankala* in parts of East Africa, and *Ohoro* elsewhere. While there are different versions of the game, each includes two players and begins with four seeds placed in each of the twelve cups (forty-eight total seeds). The object of the game is to capture as many seeds as possible. Fancier versions of the gameboard have a seed "bank" for each player on the ends of the board. When using egg cartons, the seeds can be placed on the ground or table next to the carton or in paper cups.

To begin, the two players face each other with the board between them as shown below:

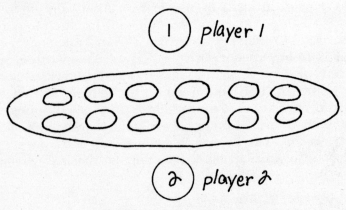

A GOOD SOUP ATTRACTS CHAIRS

Each player has the six cups nearest him or her as home base. The first player picks up the four seeds in any cup on his or her side, then places one seed in the cup to the right of it (counter-clockwise), and to the right of that one, and that one, and that one, until all four seeds are gone.

**Version I:** After he or she "plants" her fourth seed, the player scoops up the five seeds in that cup, skips over it, and continues distributing them counterclockwise around the board as before. The player continues in this manner, planting seeds and picking up the seeds in the cup in which he or she drops the last seed (always leaving it empty and planting the first seed to the right of that cup) until one of two things happens: (a) he or she drops the last seed into an empty cup, ending his or her turn, or (b) he or she drops the last seed into a cup that already had three pieces, making a total of four seeds. When "a" happens, the player's turn is over. When "b" happens, the player's turn is over, but he or she collects the four seeds in the cup where the player planted the last seed. However, if the player drops a fourth seed into a cup when it is not the last seed, the four seeds in that cup go to the opponent's bank (whether the cup is on the player's side or the opponent's side), even if the player's turn is not over. When the first player's turn is over, the opponent can begin from any of the cups on his or her own side of the board. The players continue taking turns and capturing seeds until all of the seeds are in the banks. The same player who collects the next to last four seeds, wins the last four seeds as well.

**Version II:** After the first player has planted four seeds, the second player then does the same thing—that is, pick up the seeds in any of the cups on his or her row and distribute them into the cups to the right, one at a time, until they are all gone. The players continue in this manner, taking turns picking up the seeds in one cup and distributing all of them. The goal of the game is still to try to capture as many of the other player's seeds as possible and put them in your "bank." The two ways of capturing seeds are: (a) When the last seed lands in the opponent's cup (but not a cup on your own home base) that already has only one or two seeds, you may put those seeds in your bank; or (b) Moving backwards from the last cup you put a seed in, you can collect seeds from any consecutive cup or cups (cups next to each other) that have only two or three seeds. In this version, the game ends when one player has twenty-four seeds in his or her bank, or when no player can move.

There are many other great African games—from clapping to singing to running games. Go to the local library and look for books on international games for some ideas.

### CRAFTS:

Maybe you would like to get your friends involved in making some African crafts. Tie-dye and batik are just two of the many traditional African crafts that are fun to do. Try tie-dying t-shirts in bright colors and cheerful designs. Experiment with making beads from salt dough or macaroni. Try sponge-painting or potato-painting some of the famous African designs you see in this book, like the *gye nyame* ("Except for God, I fear no one"), or the "sun and moon" (a symbol of faithfulness), or the ram's horns. Make a pattern of the symbol, and stamp it onto cloth like they do to make the adinkra cloth in Ghana.

A helpful source for ideas is *African Crafts* by Judith Hoffman Corwin (New York/London/Toronto/Sydney: Franklin Watts, 1990. 48 pages).

Just be sure to have a terrific time and enjoy yourself at your party. Good times and good friends and good African food go well together. Remember, "A good soup attracts chairs."

# Where to Learn More About African Cooking

Some good books for learning about African foods and cooking that are not too hard to find are:

*African Cooking* by Laurens van der Post and the editors of Time-Life Books. New York: Time-Life Books, 1970. (208 and 144 pages)
   This is part of the Time-Life Foods of the World series and has two books, one with just recipes and one with wonderful photographs and information.

*The Africa News Cookbook: African Cooking for Western Kitchens* edited by Tami Hultman and the Africa News Service, Inc. New York: Viking Penguin Books, 1985. (175 pages)

*The Von Welanetz Guide to Ethnic Ingredients* by Diana and Paul von Welanetz. New York: Warner Books, Inc., 1982. (722 pages)

*A West African Cook Book* by Ellen Gibson Wilson. New York: M. Evans and Company, Inc., 1971. (267 pages)

*Cooking the African Way* by Constance Nabwire and Bertha Vining Montgomery. Minneapolis: Lerner Publications Company, 1988.
   This book is part of the Easy Menu Ethnic series published by Lerner Publications. They also have a book called *Cooking the Caribbean Way* that is good to look at because there are many similarities between West Indian and West African cooking. To learn why this is so, and also why our own Southern cooking owes so much to West Africa, two interesting articles written a long time ago are:

"Peaceful Integration: The Owner's Adoption of His Slaves' Food" by Mary Tolford Wilson. *Journal of Negro History*, Vol. XLIX, No. 2 (April 1964):116-27.

"What Has Africa Given America?" by Melville J. Herskovits. *The New Republic*, Vol. LXXXIV , No. 1085 (1935).

This is reprinted on pages 168-74 of *The New World Negro,* edited by Frances S. Herskovits. Bloomington: Indiana University Press, 1966.

I am grateful to Ellen Gibson Wilson for pointing these two articles out in *A West African Cook Book.*

Three interesting books have come out recently that include a lot of African recipes. They are:

*Extending the Table: A World Community Cookbook* by Joetta Handrich Schlabach. Scottdale/Waterloo: Herald Press, 1991. (336 pages)

*Kwanzaa: An African-American Celebration of Culture and Cooking* by Eric V. Copage. New York: William Morrow and Company, Inc., 1991. (356 pages)

Copage's book also includes a section on mail order sources for obtaining special ingredients.

*Iron Pots and Wooden Spoons: Africa's Gifts to New World Cooking* by Jessica B. Harris. New York: Atheneum, 1989. (195 pages)

Some other books are helpful, but they may be harder to find. They are:

*The African Cookbook* by Bea Sandler. New York: World Publishing Company, 1972. (236 pages)

*The Best Kept Secrets of West and East African Cooking* by Ola Olaore. London: W. Foulsham & Company, Ltd., 1980. (96 pages)

This may not be too difficult to find since it was re-released in hardback in 1990 as *Traditional African Cooking.*

*Black Africa Cookbook* by Monica Bayley. San Francisco: Determined Productions, Inc., 1977. (125 pages)

*Ghanaian Favourite Dishes* by Alice Dede. Accra: Anowuo Educational Publications, 1969. (104 pages)

*Ghana Recipe Book* by E. Chapman Nyaho, E. Amarteifio, and J. Asare. Accra-Tema: Ghana Publishing Corporation, 1970. (140 pages)

*The Kudeti Book of Yoruba Cookery* by J. A. Mars and E. M. Tooleyo. Lagos: C.S.S. Bookshops, 1979. (60 pages)

*Many Hands Cooking: An International Cookbook for Girls and Boys* by Terry Cooper and Marilyn Ratner. New York: Y. Crowell (in cooperation with the U.S. Committee for UNICEF), 1974. (50 pages)

*Nigerian Cookbook* by H. O. Anthonio and M. Isoun. London: Macmillan, 1982. (216 pages)

*Nourishing Ways With Tropical Fruits* by Ada Nnena Amoji.

This thirty-page booklet by a Nigerian caterer and nutritionist has no date or publisher listed.

*A Safari of African Cooking* by Bill Odarty. Detroit: Broadside Press, 1971. (137 pages)

This also may not be too hard to find—a second edition was published in 1987, and another in 1991.

*Tropical Leaf Vegetables in Human Nutrition* by H. A. P. C. Oomen and G. J. H. Grubben. Amsterdam and Curacao: Royal Tropical Institute and Orphan Publishing Company, 1977. (140 pages)

Printed in the United States
4412